AUTHENTIC TRANSCRIPTIONS WITH NOTES AND TABLATURE

BEST OF ANTHRAX

Cover photo: Morrison/RETNA LTD

Music transcriptions by Pete Billmann, Addi Booth, Ron Piccione, and David Stocker

ISBN 978-1-4234-1406-3

7777 W. BLUEMOUND RD. P.O. BOX 13819 MILWAUKEE, WI 53213

Visit Hal Leonard Online at
www.halleonard.com

from *Spreading the Disease*

A.I.R.

Words and Music by Joseph Bellardini, Frank Bello, Charlie Benante, Scott Rosenfeld and Daniel Spitz

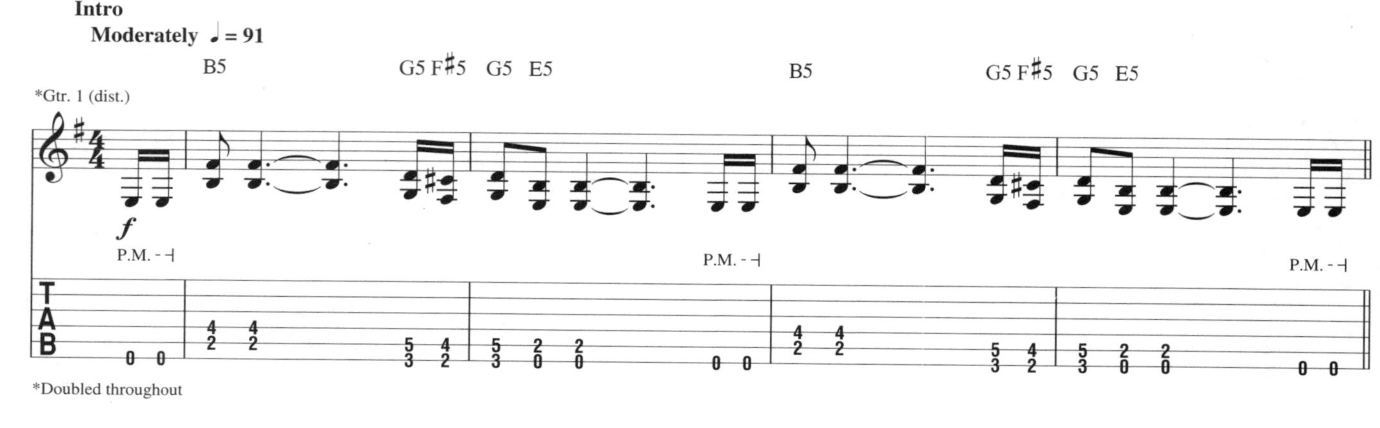

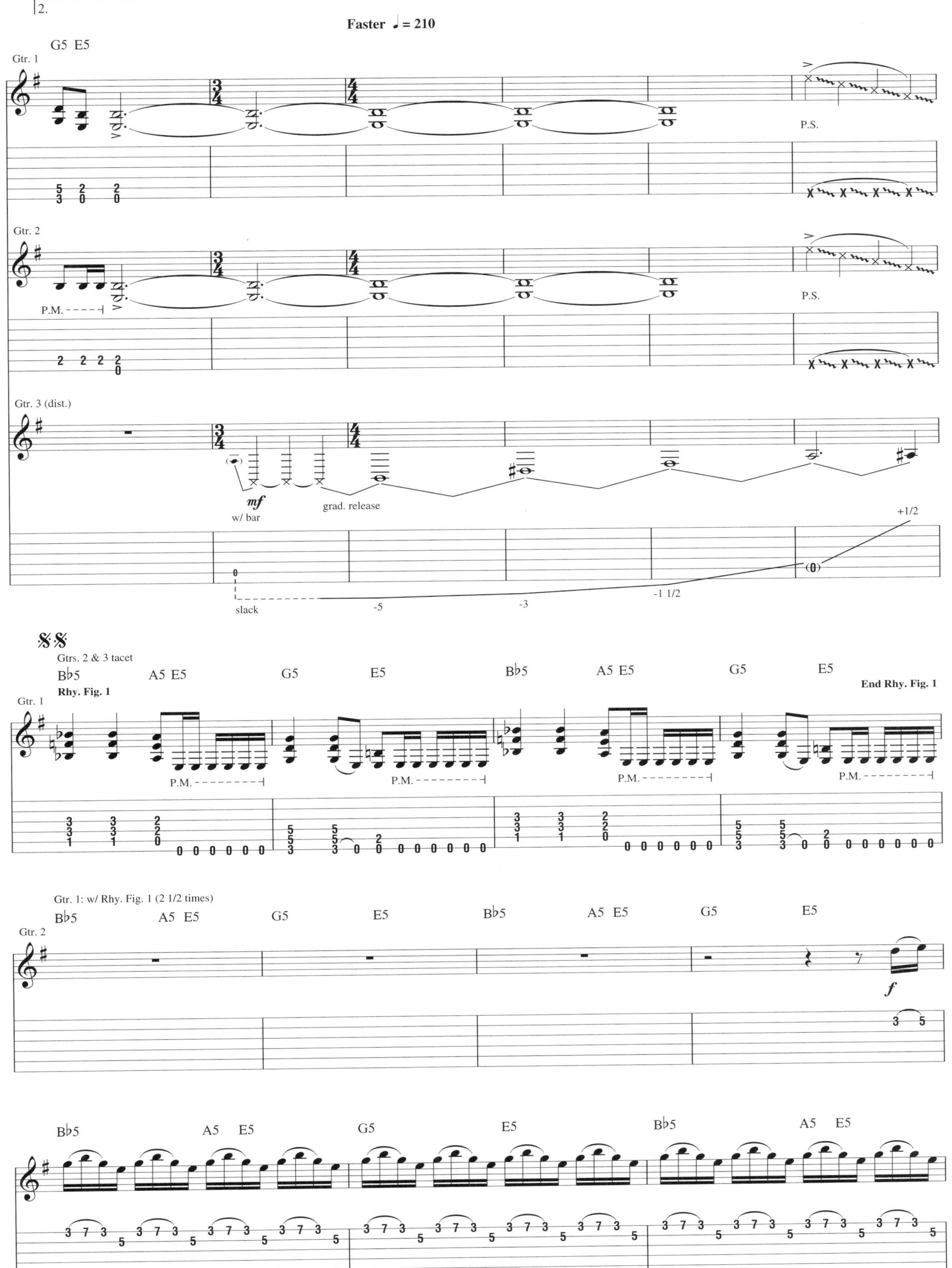

2.
Faster ♩ = 210
G5 E5
Gtr. 1
P.S.
Gtr. 2
P.M.
P.S.
Gtr. 3 (dist.)
mf
w/ bar
grad. release
+1/2
slack
-5
-3
-1 1/2
Gtrs. 2 & 3 tacet
B♭5 A5 E5 G5 E5 B♭5 A5 E5 G5 E5
Rhy. Fig. 1
End Rhy. Fig. 1
Gtr. 1
P.M.
Gtr. 1: w/ Rhy. Fig. 1 (2 1/2 times)
B♭5 A5 E5 G5 E5 B♭5 A5 E5 G5 E5
Gtr. 2
f
B♭5 A5 E5 G5 E5 B♭5 A5 E5

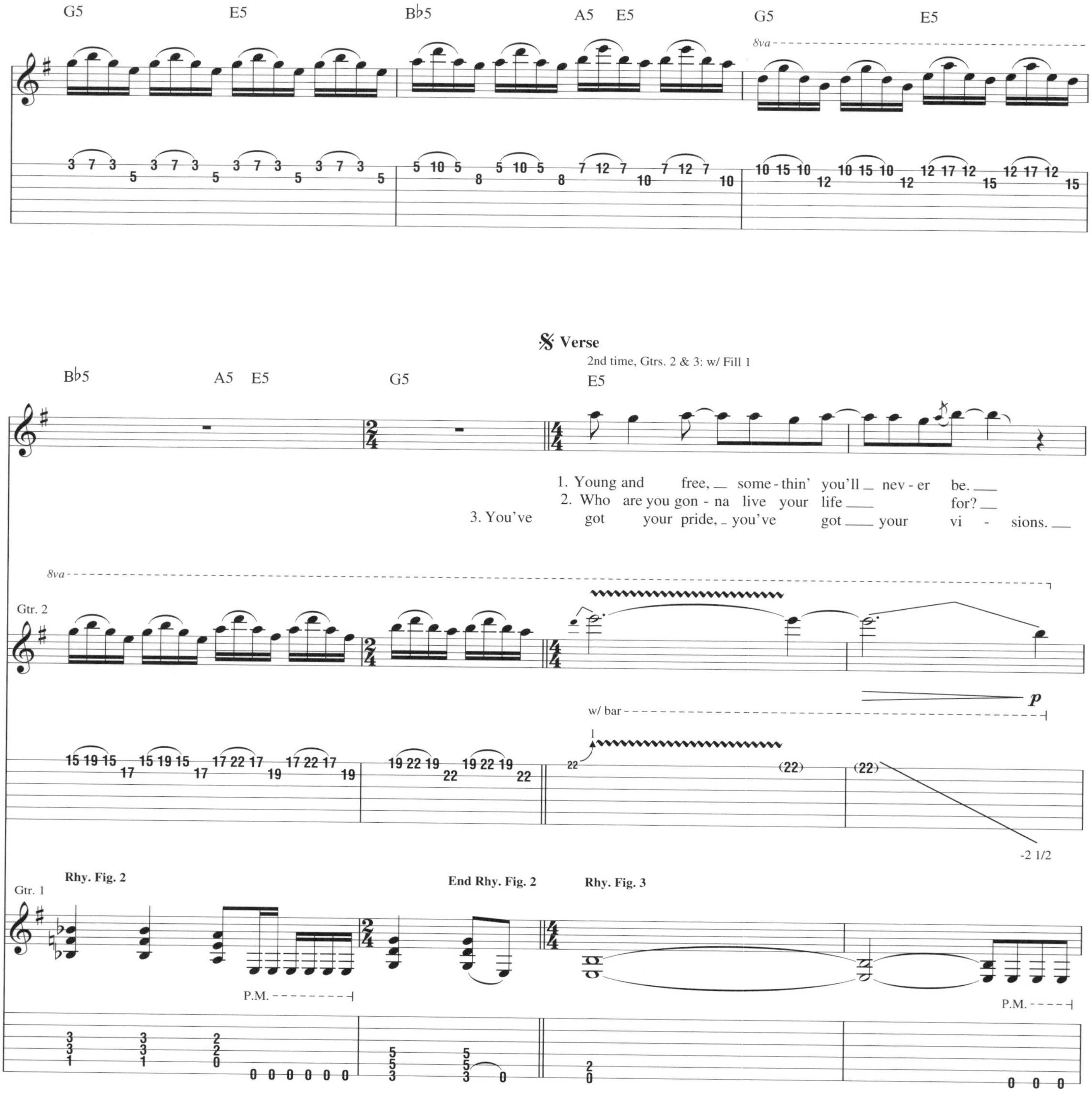

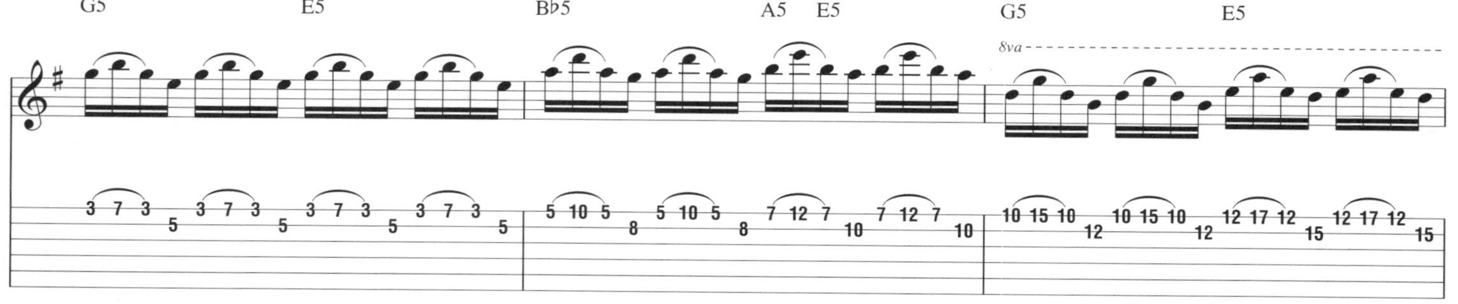

𝄋 Verse

2nd time, Gtrs. 2 & 3: w/ Fill 1

B♭5 A5 E5 G5 E5

1. Young and free, __ some - thin' you'll __ nev - er be. __
2. Who are you gon - na live your life __ for? __
3. You've got your pride, _ you've got __ your vi - sions. __

8va

Gtr. 2

p

w/ bar

-2 1/2

Rhy. Fig. 2

Gtr. 1

P.M.

End Rhy. Fig. 2

Rhy. Fig. 3

P.M.

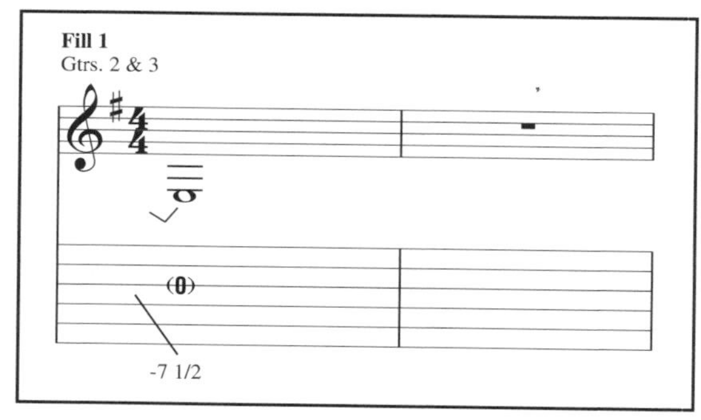

Gtr. 2 tacet
B♭5
A5
E5
G5
At
Con -
Gtr. 1
End Rhy. Fig. 3
P.M.
Gtr. 1: w/ Rhy. Fig. 3 (2 2/3 times)
child - hood's end it's lu - na - cy.
form - i - ty will trap you like a locked door.
Don't sub - side, don't ev - er give in,
no.
Pure dic - ta - tion, they don't lis - ten.
In - de - pend - ence means own - in' your de - ci - sions.
Don't com - pro - mise, just keep on win - nin'.
To Coda 2
You just wait for what you're miss - in', oh.
Au - thor - i - ty will put your soul in pris - on.
The games they play, you just keep on win - nin'.
Rhy. Fig. 4
End Rhy. Fig. 4

Chorus
E5
E7(no3rd)
E5
E7(no3rd)
E5
E7(no3rd)
Wel - come to your night - mare, _
Rhy. Fig. 5
P.M.
E5 Eb5 D5 Db5 C5
D5
just can't walk a - way. _
It's time for you _
End Rhy. Fig. 5
P.M.
Gtr. 1: w/ Rhy. Fig. 5 (1 2/3 times)
E5 E7(no3rd) E5 E7(no3rd) E5 E7(no3rd) E5 Eb5 D5 Db5 C5
_ to choose _ your fate. _ You just can't let it lay. _
D5 E5 E7(no3rd) E5 E7(no3rd) E5 E7(no3rd) E5 Eb5 D5 Db5 C5
_ Wel - come to { our / your } night - mare. Your whole life's on the way _
B5
to - day. _
Gtr. 1
P.M.

E5
B5 E5
B5 E5
B5 A5
You're no good, mis-un-der-stood, a. i. r.
Rhy. Fig. 6
End Rhy. Fig. 6
P.M.
Gtr. 1: w/ Rhy. Fig. 6 (2 3/4 times)
All their hopes and vi - sions of what they want you to be.
Cru - cial times, made up minds, a. i. r.
So high and might - y, they're
To Coda 1
B5 A5 G5 E5
much too blind to see.
Gtr. 1
Interlude
Gtr. 1: w/ Rhy. Fig. 1 (1 1/2 times)
B♭5 A5 E5 G5 E5 B♭5 A5 E5 G5 E5
Gtrs. 2 & 3
8va
w/ bar
grad. release
Harm.
w/ bar
Pitch: G

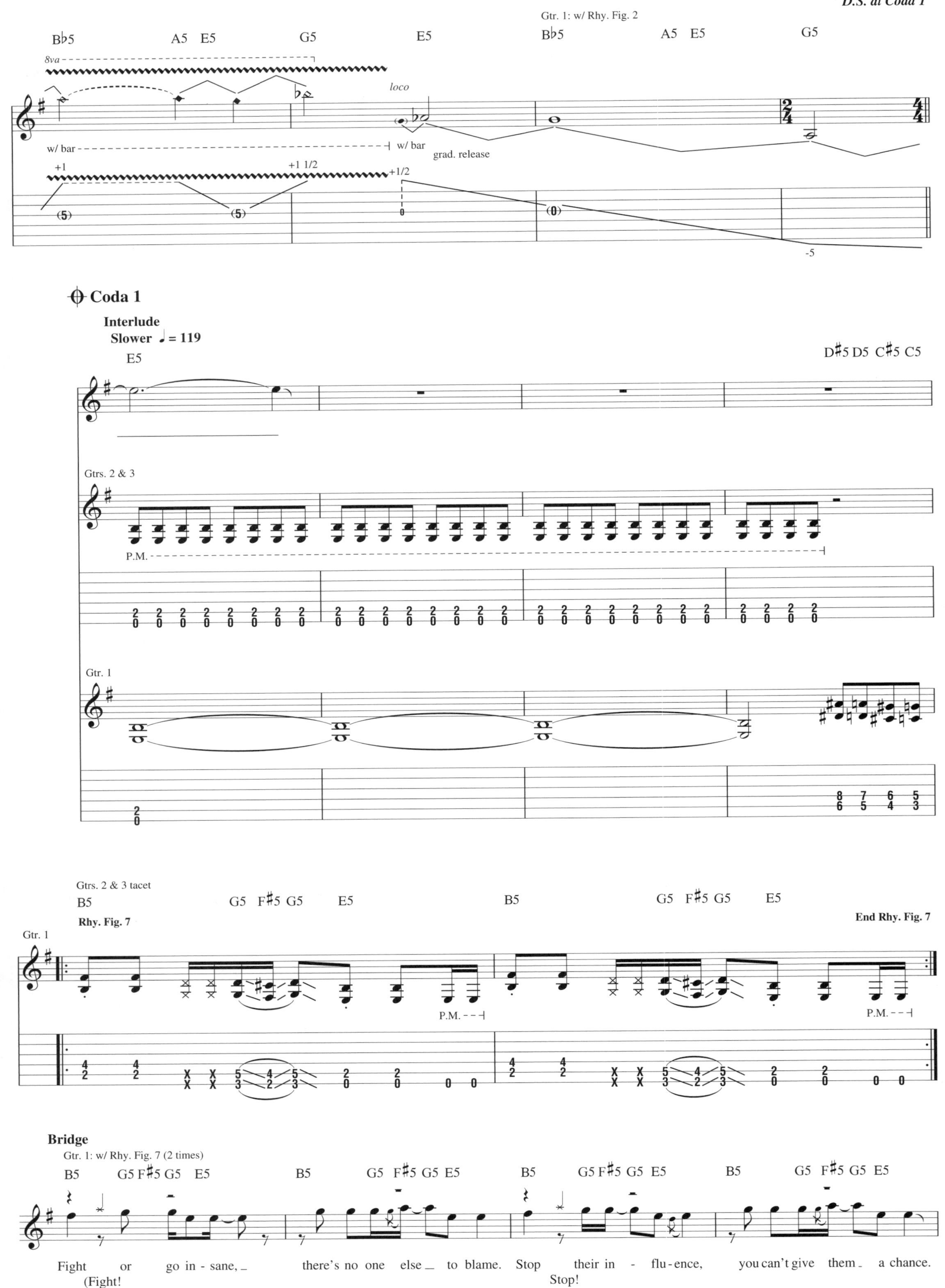
D.S. al Coda 1
Gtr. 1: w/ Rhy. Fig. 2
B♭5
A5
E5
G5
E5
B♭5
A5
E5
G5
8va
loco
w/ bar
w/ bar
grad. release
Coda 1
Interlude
Slower ♩ = 119
E5
D♯5 D5 C♯5 C5
Gtrs. 2 & 3
P.M.
Gtr. 1
Gtrs. 2 & 3 tacet
B5
G5 F♯5 G5
E5
B5
G5 F♯5 G5
E5
Rhy. Fig. 7
End Rhy. Fig. 7
Gtr. 1
P.M.
Bridge
Gtr. 1: w/ Rhy. Fig. 7 (2 times)
B5
G5 F♯5 G5
E5
Fight or go in - sane, there's no one else to blame. Stop their in - flu - ence, you can't give them a chance.
(Fight!
Stop!

C♯5 A5 G♯5 A5 F♯5 C♯5 A5 G♯5 A5 F♯5
Break right through the wall. It sep - a - rates us all.
Break!
Gtr. 1
Rhy. Fig. 8
End Rhy. Fig. 8
P.M.
Gtr. 1: w/ Rhy. Fig. 8
C♯5 A5 G♯5 A5 F♯5 C♯5 A5 G♯5 A5 F♯5
Start your sec-ond life with-out their hands in sight.
Start!)
Gtr. 2
P.M.
Guitar Solo
Gtr. 1: w/ Rhy. Fig. 7 (2 times)
B5 G5 F♯5 G5 E5 B5 G5 F♯5 G5 E5
B5 G5 F♯5 G5 E5 B5 G5 F♯5 G5 E5
8va
P.M.

Gtr. 1: w/ Rhy. Fig. 8 (2 times)
C♯5
A5 G♯5 A5
F♯5
Gtr. 2 tacet
C♯5
A5 G♯5 A5
F♯5
8va
Gtr. 2
Gtr. 3
loco
slight P.H.
P.M.
C♯5
A5 G♯5 A5
F♯5
C♯5
A5 G♯5 A5
F♯5
8va
Gtr. 3
w/ bar
-1 1/2
Gtr. 1: w/ Rhy. Fig. 7
Gtr. 3 tacet
B5
G5 F♯5 G5
E5
B5
G5 F♯5 G5
E5
Gtr. 2
P.M.
B5
G5 F♯5 G5
E5
B5
G5 F♯5 G5
E5
Gtr. 2
P.M.
w/ bar
-4 1/2
slack
Gtr. 1
P.M.

Faster ♩ = 212
D.S.S. al Coda 2
Gtr. 2 tacet
Ow!
Gtr. 1
P.M.
Coda 2
Outro
Gtr. 1: w/ Rhy. Fig. 4
Gtr. 1: w/ Rhy. Fig. 4 (2 times)
B♭5 A5 E5 G5 E5
Keep on win - nin',
B♭5 A5 E5 G5 F♯5 E5
keep on win - nin',
Rhy. Fig. 9
End Rhy. Fig. 9
Gtr. 1: w/ Rhy. Fig. 9
keep on win - nin'.
A. I. R.

from *State of Euphoria*

Be All End All

Words and Music by Joseph Bellardini, Frank Bello, Charlie Benante, Scott Rosenfeld and Daniel Spitz

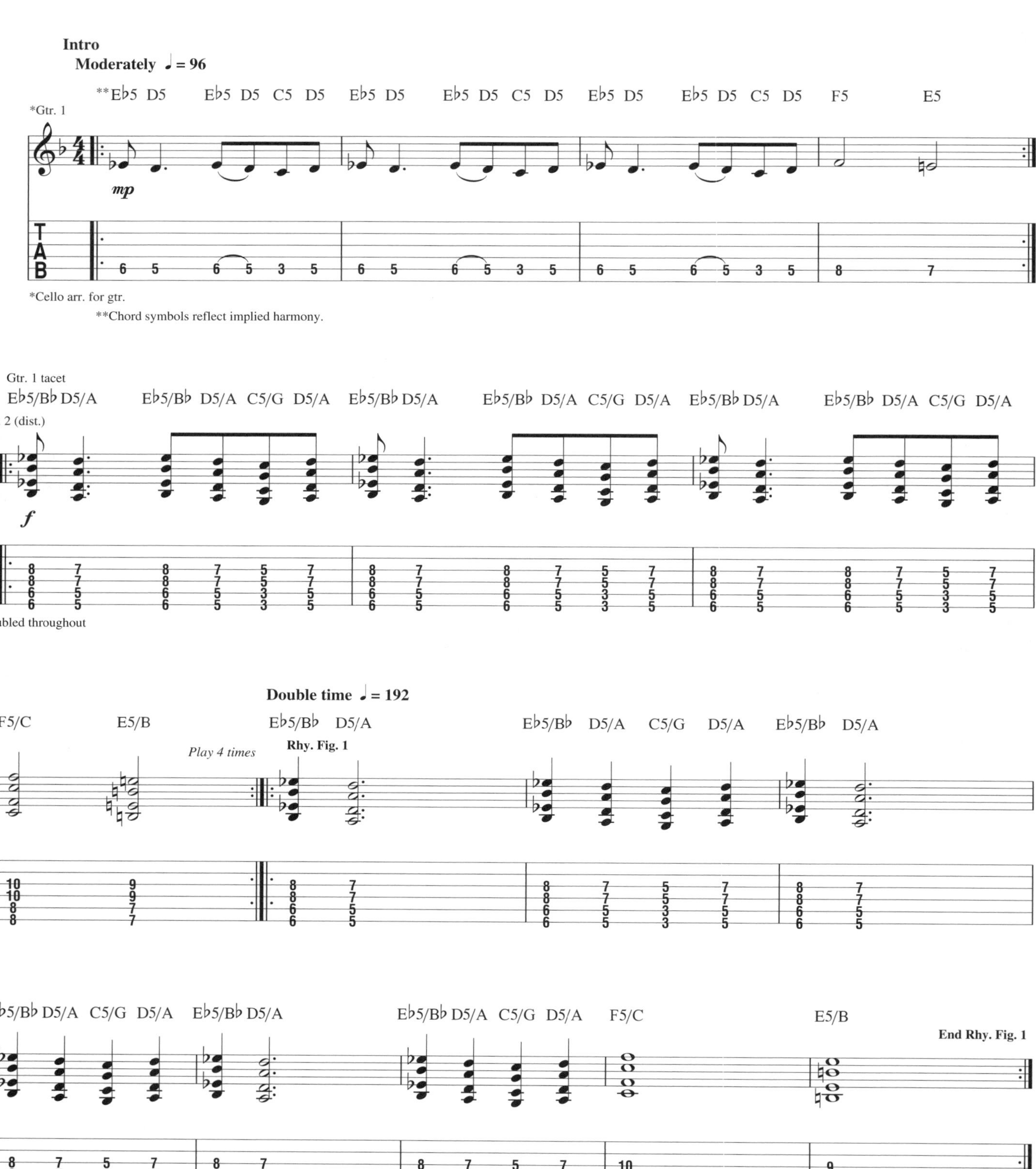

E5
Yes, no, yes, no.
P.M.
Verse
Bb5 A5 Bb5 A5 G5 A5 Bb5 A5 Bb5 A5 G5 A5
1. Not an - oth - er word. You knew what to do.
2. Think on your feet and stay one step a - head.
Rhy. Fig. 2
End Rhy. Fig. 2
P.M.
F5 E5 F5 E5 D5 E5 F5 E5 F5 E5 D5 E5
Right in your face they see it. In their face you
Break! Take your brain and use it. Take their mind and
P.M.
Gtr. 2: w/ Rhy. Fig. 2
Bb5 A5 Bb5 A5 G5 A5 Bb5 A5 Bb5A5 G5 A5
take it. Make up their minds, ag - gres - sion turns the screw.
change an at - ti - tude like you change your shorts.

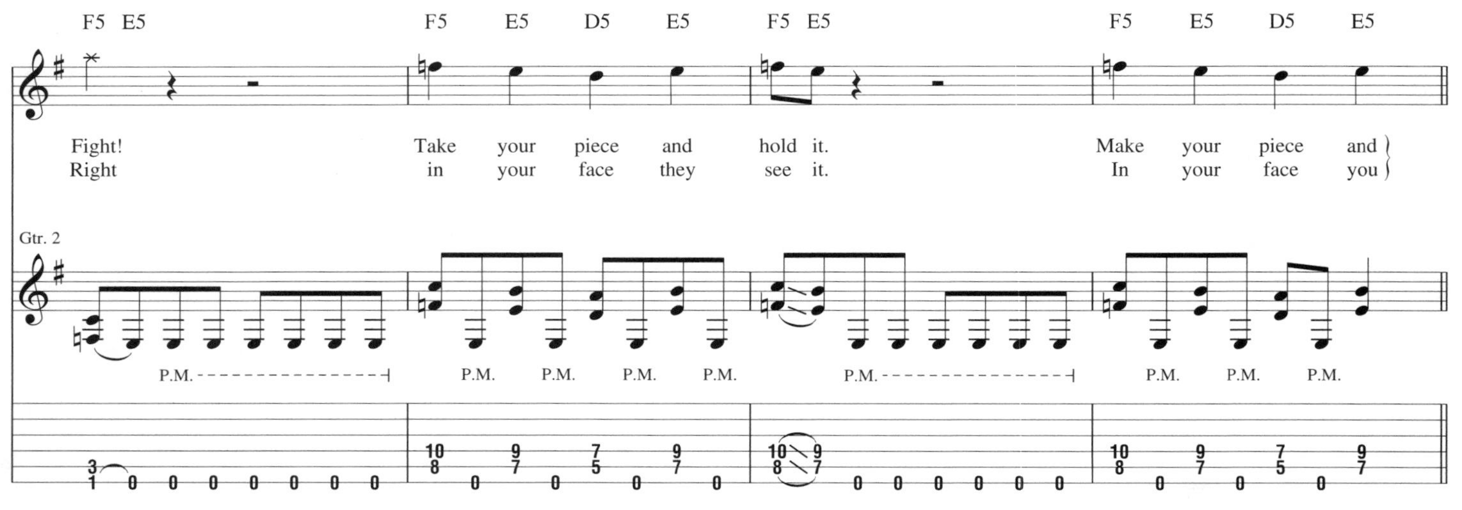
F5 E5
F5 E5 D5 E5
F5 E5
F5 E5 D5 E5
Fight! Take your piece and hold it. Make your piece and
Right in your face they see it. In your face you
Gtr. 2
P.M.

Pre-Chorus
G5 E5 F5 C5 B5 E5
stand up. You know what it means.
Rhy. Fig. 3
End Rhy. Fig. 3
P.M.
Gtr. 2: w/ Rhy. Fig. 3
Wake up, time to live your dreams.

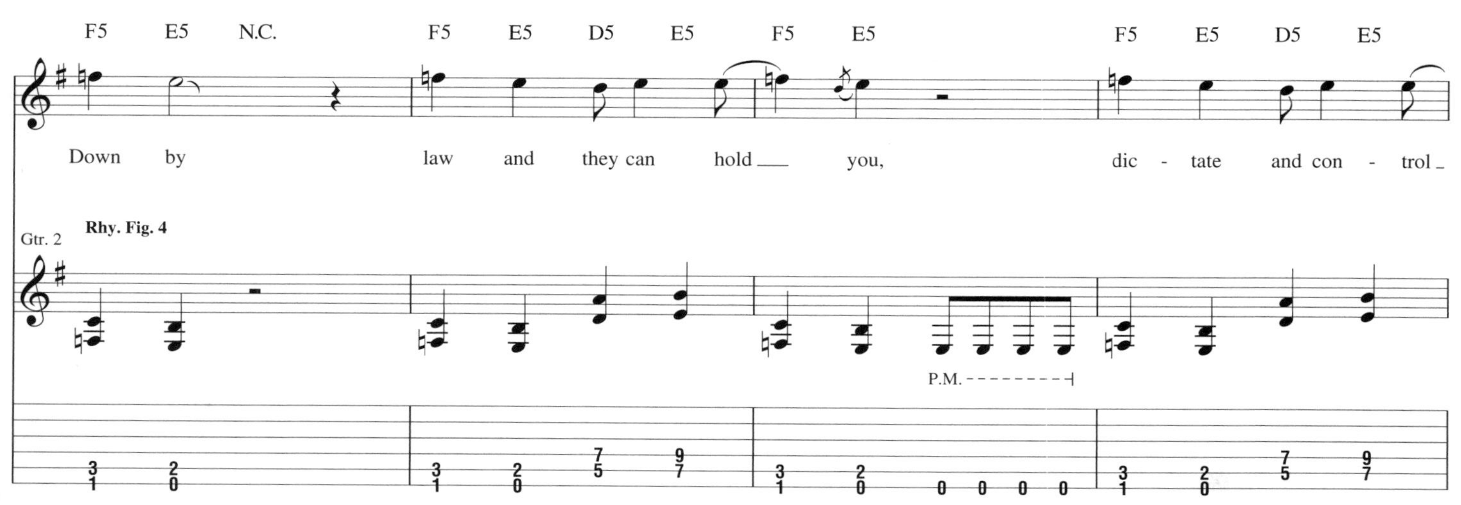
F5 E5 N.C.
F5 E5 D5 E5
Down by law and they can hold you, dic - tate and con - trol
Gtr. 2
Rhy. Fig. 4
P.M.

F5 E5 N.C. F5 E5 D5 E5 C5 B5
you, hold on to your i - de - as.
End Rhy. Fig. 4
Gtr. 2: w/ Rhy. Fig. 4
F5 E5 N.C. F5 E5 D5 E5 F5 E5 F5 E5 D5 E5
Down by law and no one owns you, all the shit they've thrown
F5 E5 N.C. F5 E5 D5 E5 C5 B5
you. Pay - back is a real bitch.
F5 G5 B♭5 A5 B♭5 A5 F5 G5 B♭5 A5 B♭5 A5
Noth-ing's ev - er eas - y when you do it your - self. All that you can do is try.
Gtr. 2
Rhy. Fig. 5
End Rhy. Fig. 5
P.M.
Gtr. 2: w/ Rhy. Fig. 5
F5 G5 B♭5 A5 B♭5 A5 F5 G5 B♭5 A5 B♭5 A5
Life's not un - fair, life is life. Death, not su - i - cide.
Chorus
Gtr. 2: w/ Rhy. Fig. 1 (2 times)
E♭5/B♭ D5/A E♭5/B♭ D5/A C5/G D5/A E♭5/B♭ D5/A E♭5/B♭ D5/A C5/G D5/A
Be all, and you'll be the end all. Life can be a real

Eb5/Bb D5/A Eb5/Bb D5/A C5/G D5/A F5/C E5/B
ball. State of mind, eu - phor - i - a.
Eb5/Bb D5/A Eb5/Bb D5/A C5/G D5/A Eb5/Bb D5/A Eb5/Bb D5/A C5/G D5/A
Be all, and you'll be the end all. Life can be a real
Eb5/Bb D5/A Eb5/Bb D5/A C5/G D5/A F5/C E5/B
ball. State of mind, eu - phor - i - a.
1., 2.
Interlude
Slower ♩ = 179
E5
Gtr. 2
P.M.
3.
G5 E5 F5 C5 B5
E5

Bridge
G5 F5 C5 B5 E5 F5 E5
Al - ways tak - ing, al - ways fak - ing.
Riff A
End Riff A
P.M.
Gtr. 2: w/ Riff A (2 times)
G5 F5 C5 B5 E5 F5 E5 G5 F5 C5 B5 E5 F5 E5
Ig - no - rance is so frus - trat - ing. Al - ways tak - ing, al - ways fak - ing.
G5 F5 C5 F5 E5 F5 E5 F5 E5 F5 E5
Ig - no - rance is no way, no way, no way, no way
Gtr. 2
Guitar Solo
Faster ♩ = 213
F5 D5 E5 F5 D5 E5 F5 D5 E5 F5 D5 E5
out!
Gtr. 3 (dist.)
f
Rhy. Fig. 6
Gtr. 2
P.M.

F5 D5 E5
F5 D5 E5
G5
F♯5
End Rhy. Fig. 6
P.M.
P.M.
Gtr. 2: w/ Rhy. Fig. 6
Gtr. 3
grad. bend
Gtr. 4 (dist.)
mf
Gtr. 3
Gtr. 2
Rhy. Fig. 7
F5 E5
E5
P.M.

E5 F5 E5 F5 C5 B5

End Rhy. Fig. 7

P.M.

Gtr. 2: w/ Rhy. Fig. 7 (3 times)

F5 E5 F5 E5 F5 E5 F5 E5 F5

Gtr. 4

Gtr. 3

E5 F5 E5 F5 C5 B5
Gtr. 4 tacet
F5 E5 F5 E5 F5 E5
Gtr. 3
F5 E5 F5 E5 F5 E5 F5
C5 B5 F5 E5
8va

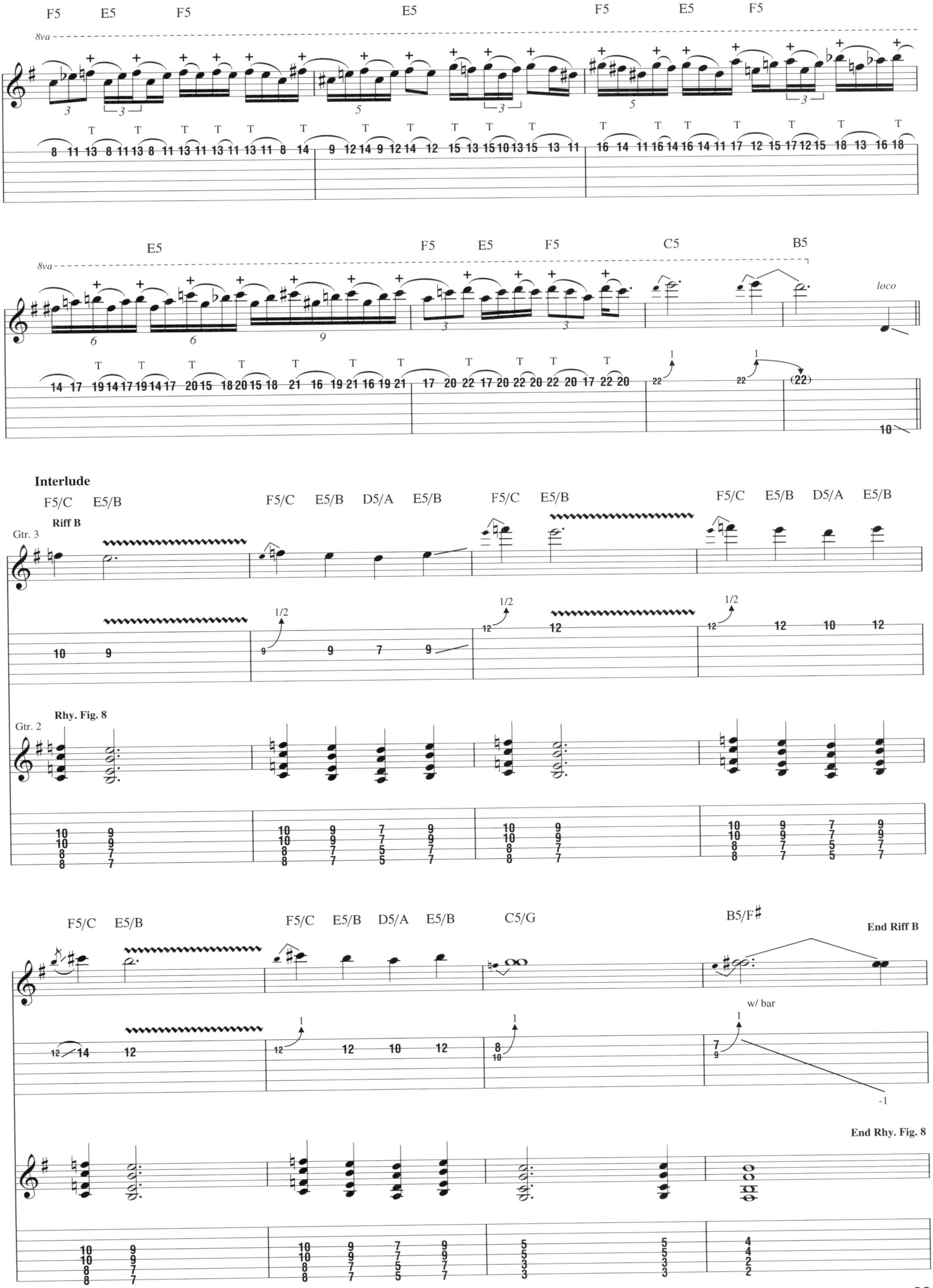

F5 E5 F5 E5 F5 E5 F5

8va

E5 F5 E5 F5 C5 B5

8va

loco

Interlude

F5/C E5/B F5/C E5/B D5/A E5/B F5/C E5/B F5/C E5/B D5/A E5/B

Riff B

Gtr. 3

1/2 1/2 1/2

Rhy. Fig. 8

Gtr. 2

Gtr. 2: w/ Rhy. Fig. 8 (2 times)
Gtr. 3: w/ Riff B (1 1/2 times)
F5/C E5/B F5/C E5/B D5/A E5/B F5/C E5/B F5/C E5/B D5/A E5/B
(Oh.
F5/C E5/B F5/C E5/B D5/A E5/B C5/G B5/F♯
F5/C E5/B F5/C E5/B D5/A E5/B F5/C E5/B F5/C E5/B D5/A E5/B
Oh.)
F5/C E5/B F5/C E5/B D5/A E5/B C5/G B5/F♯
Gtr. 3
8va
Chorus
Gtr. 2: w/ Rhy. Fig. 1 (2 times)
Gtr. 3 tacet
E♭5/B♭ D5/A E♭5/B♭ D5/A C5/G D5/A E♭5/B♭ D5/A E♭5/B♭ D5/A C5/G D5/A
Be all, and you'll be the end all. Life can be a real
loco
pp

E♭5/B♭ D5/A E♭5/B♭ D5/A C5/G D5/A F5/C E5/B
ball. State of mind, eu - phor - i - a.
E♭5/B♭ D5/A E♭5/B♭ D5/A C5/G D5/A E♭5/B♭ D5/A E♭5/B♭ D5/A C5/G D5/A
Be all, and you'll be the end all. Life can be a real
E♭5/B♭ D5/A E♭5/B♭ D5/A C5/G D5/A F5/C E5/B
ball. State of mind, eu - phor -
C5/G D5/A F5/C E5/B
i - a.
Gtr. 2
Outro
Slower ♩ = 180
E5/B
Gtr. 1
rit.
Gtr. 2
rit.
pp

from *Persistence of Time*

Belly of the Beast

Words and Music by Joseph Bellardini, Frank Bello, Charlie Benante, Scott Rosenfeld and Daniel Spitz

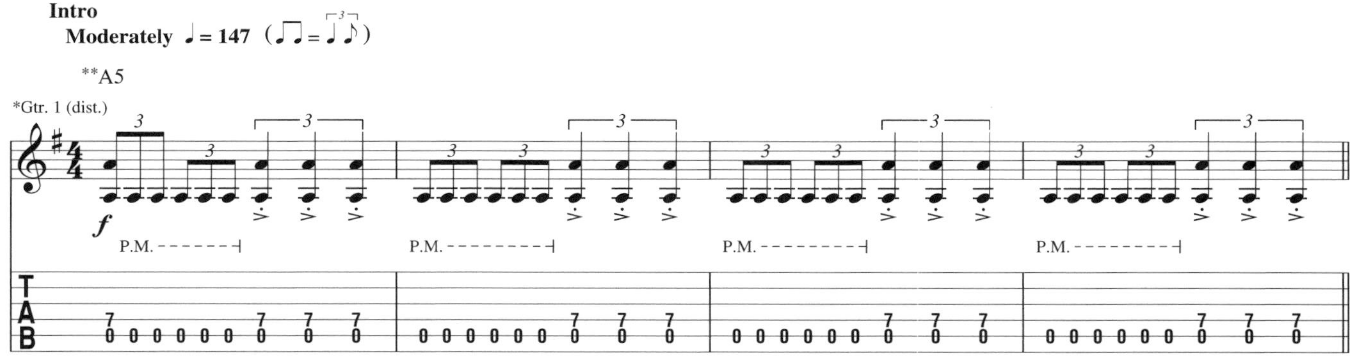

*Doubled throughout

**Chord symbols reflect implied harmony.

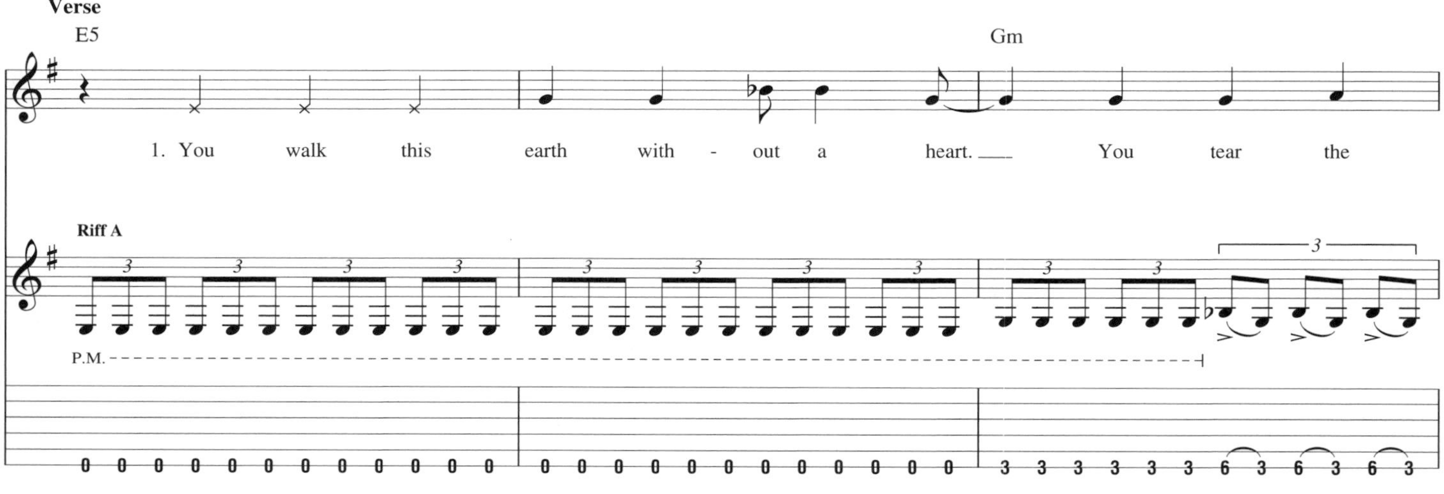

A5
You walk this earth with - out a heart. Your u - ni - form could - n't be tak - en off.
Riff B
End Riff B
P.M.
Gtr. 1: w/ Riff A
E5
Gm
A tat - too burned in - to your flesh. Your mind, your voice,
Gtr. 1: w/ Riff B
A5
these are your in - stru - ments of death. How could you dare to be so bold.
Gtr. 1: w/ Riff A
E5
You on - ly did as you were told. Mar - i - o - nettes danc - ing in time
Gm
to the a - pol - o - get - ic lines, for all the mon - sters of our time.
E5 A5 A♭5 G5 C5 B5 B♭5 G5 G♭5 F5
Gtr. 1
Rhy. Fig. 1
End Rhy. Fig. 1
P.M.

Chorus
E5
A5 A♭5 G5
C5 B5
B♭5
G5 G♭5 F5
Who is e - vil, who is blind?
In the name of who you'll find.
A
G5
cit - y of souls dy - ing for peace.
Wel - come to the bel - ly of the beast.
F5
Gr. 2
mf
P.M.
Gtr. 1

E5
G5
One mind, one voice. Wel - come to the bel - ly of the beast.
P.M.
P.H.
E5
Gtr. 2 tacet
B♭
A
E5
Who hears your voice? Mil - lions, nev - er, nev - er a - gain.
Rhy. Fig. 2
End Rhy. Fig. 2
P.M.
To Coda
Gtr. 1: w/ Rhy. Fig. 2 (2 1/2 times)
B♭
A
E5
Mad - ness, nev - er, nev - er a - gain. Mar - tyrs, dead that can't die. Mon - sters.

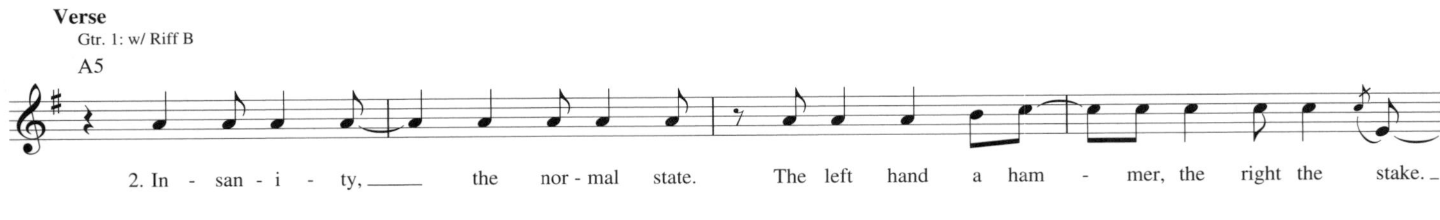
Verse
Gtr. 1: w/ Riff B
A5
2. In - san - i - ty, the nor - mal state. The left hand a ham - mer, the right the stake.

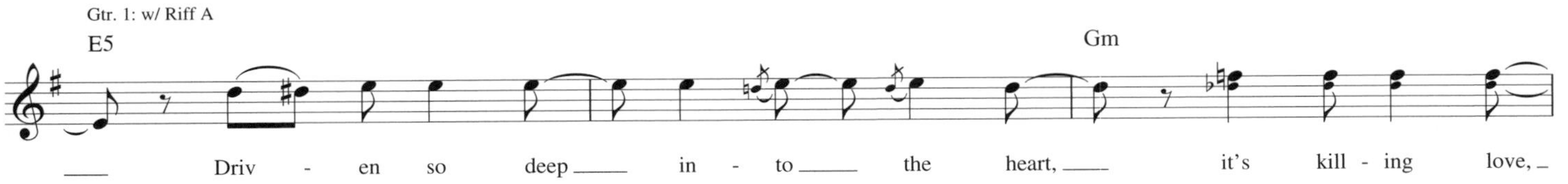
Gtr. 1: w/ Riff A
E5
Gm
Driv - en so deep in - to the heart, it's kill - ing love,

it's kill - ing faith, it's kill - ing 'cause it's from the heart.

Gtr. 1: w/ Riff B
A5
What bet - ter way to de - mor - al - ize when your own chil - dren are your spies?

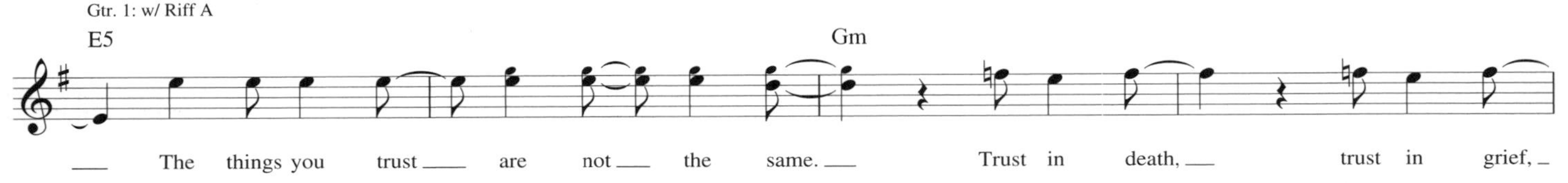
Gtr. 1: w/ Riff A
E5
Gm
The things you trust are not the same. Trust in death, trust in grief,

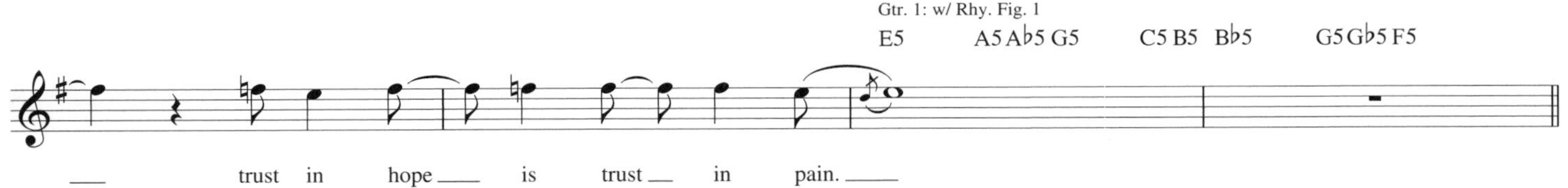
D.S. al Coda
Gtr. 1: w/ Rhy. Fig. 1
E5 A5 A♭5 G5 C5 B5 B♭5 G5 G♭5 F5
trust in hope is trust in pain.

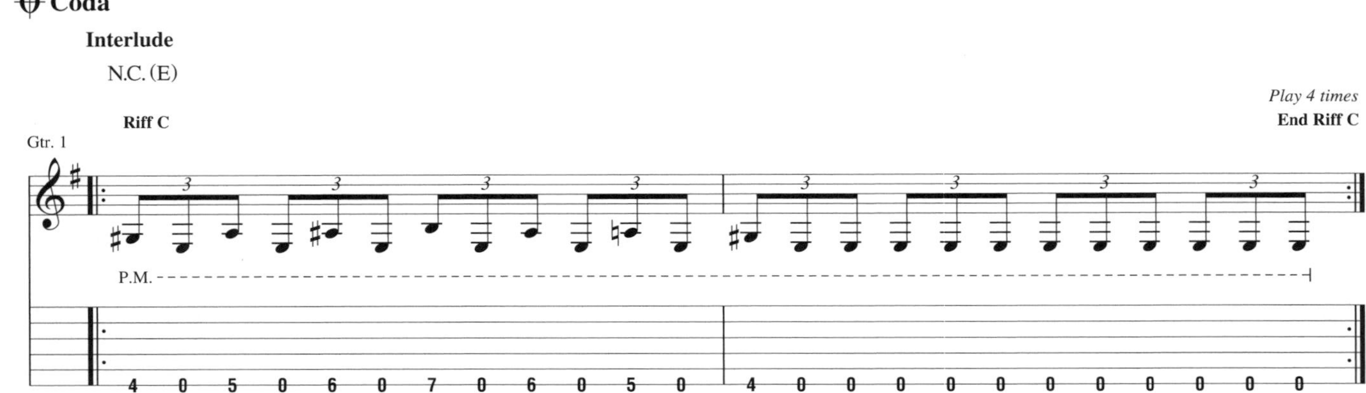
Coda
Interlude
N.C.(E)
Play 4 times
Riff C
End Riff C
Gtr. 1
P.M.
4 0 5 0 6 0 7 0 6 0 5 0 4 0 0 0 0 0 0 0 0 0 0 0

Guitar Solo
Gtr. 1: w/ Riff C (4 times)
N.C. (E)
Gtr. 3 (dist.)
w/ flanger
B♭5
A5
E5
Gtr. 3
slight
P.H.
P.M.
Gtr. 1
*w/ pitch shifter
*Set for a perfect fourth above.

Interlude
N.C. (E)
Gtr. 3 tacet
8va
w/ pitch shifter
P.M.
Gtr. 1
P.M.
G5
E5
Riff D
End Riff D
P.M.
Bridge
Gtr. 1: w/ Riff D
E5
Who is e - vil? Who is blind?
In the name of where you find.
You're

not sup - posed to ques - tion faith, but how do you ac - cept this fate?
Chorus
Bb5
A5
E5
*Voc. Fig. 1
(Mil - lions,
You walk this earth with - out a heart,
Gtr. 1
Rhy. Fig. 3
End Rhy. Fig. 3
P.M.
*Refers to downstemmed voc. only.
Gtr. 1: w/ Rhy. Fig. 3 (2 1/2 times)
End Voc. Fig. 1
mad - ness,
tear - ing in-no-cent souls a - part.
mar - tyrs,
Shov-el your con-science in-to the grave.
mon - sters.)
A
cit-y of souls dy - ing for peace.
Wel - come to the bel-ly of the beast.
Gtr. 2
Gtr. 1

G5
E5
One mind, one voice. Wel - come to the bel - ly of the beast.
Riff E1
End Riff E1
P.M.
Riff E
End Riff E
P.M.
Gtrs. 1 & 2: w/ Riffs E & E1 (2 times)
G5
E5
Who hears your voice? This is the bel - ly of the beast.
G5
E5
And all the souls dy - ing for peace in - side the bel - ly of the beast.
Bkgd. Voc.: w/ Voc. Fig. 1
Gtr. 1: w/ Rhy. Fig. 3 (3 1/2 times)
B♭5
A5
E5
Nev-er and nev-er a - gain.
B♭5
A5
E5
Nev-er and nev-er a - gain.
B♭5
A5
E5
Dead that can't die.
B♭5
A5
Outro
N.C. (E)
G5
Gtr. 1
(Cowbell)
P.M.

from *Sound of White Noise*

Black Lodge

Words and Music by Angelo Badalamenti, John Bush, Scott Rosenfeld, Frank Bello and Charlie Benante

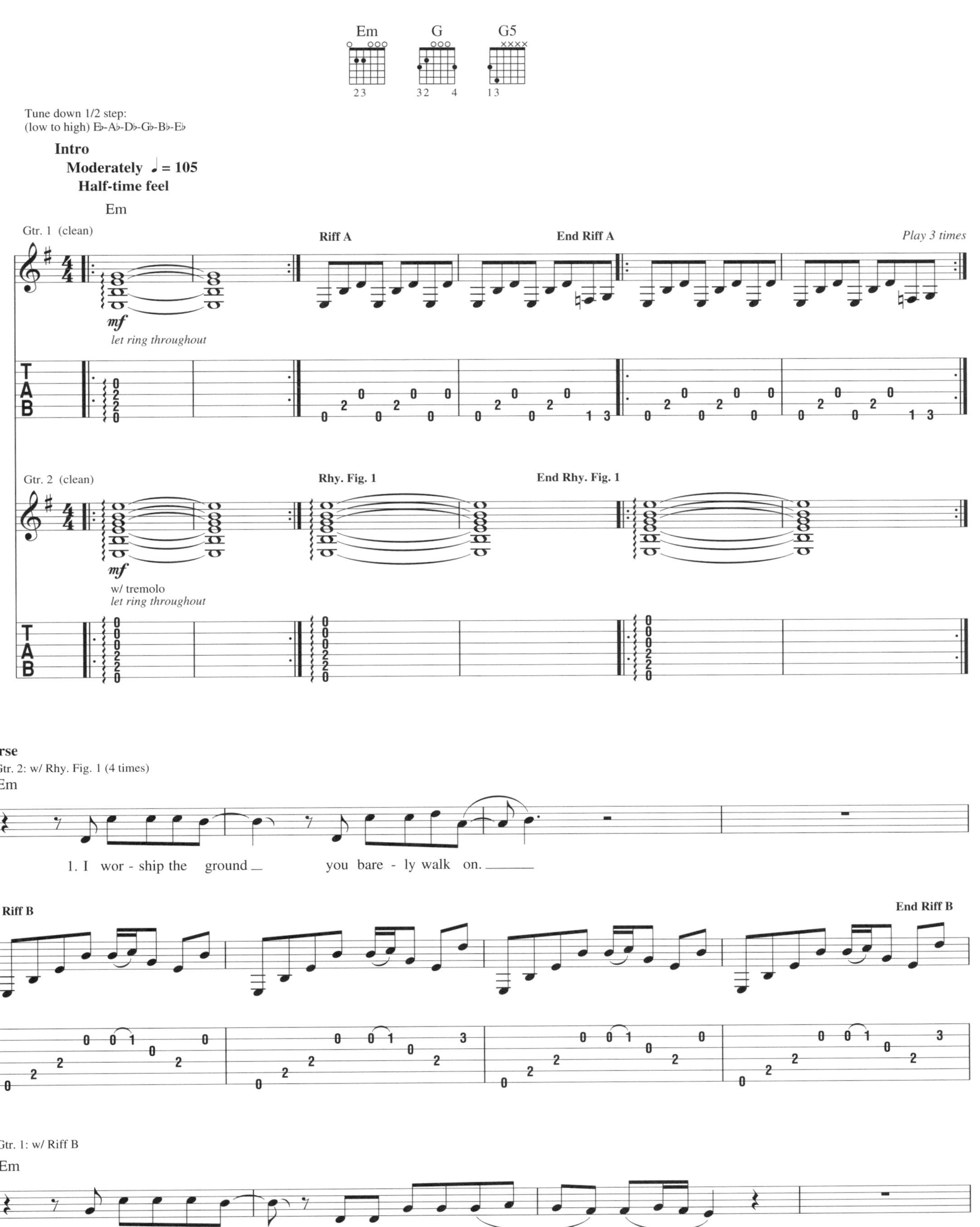

Pre-Chorus

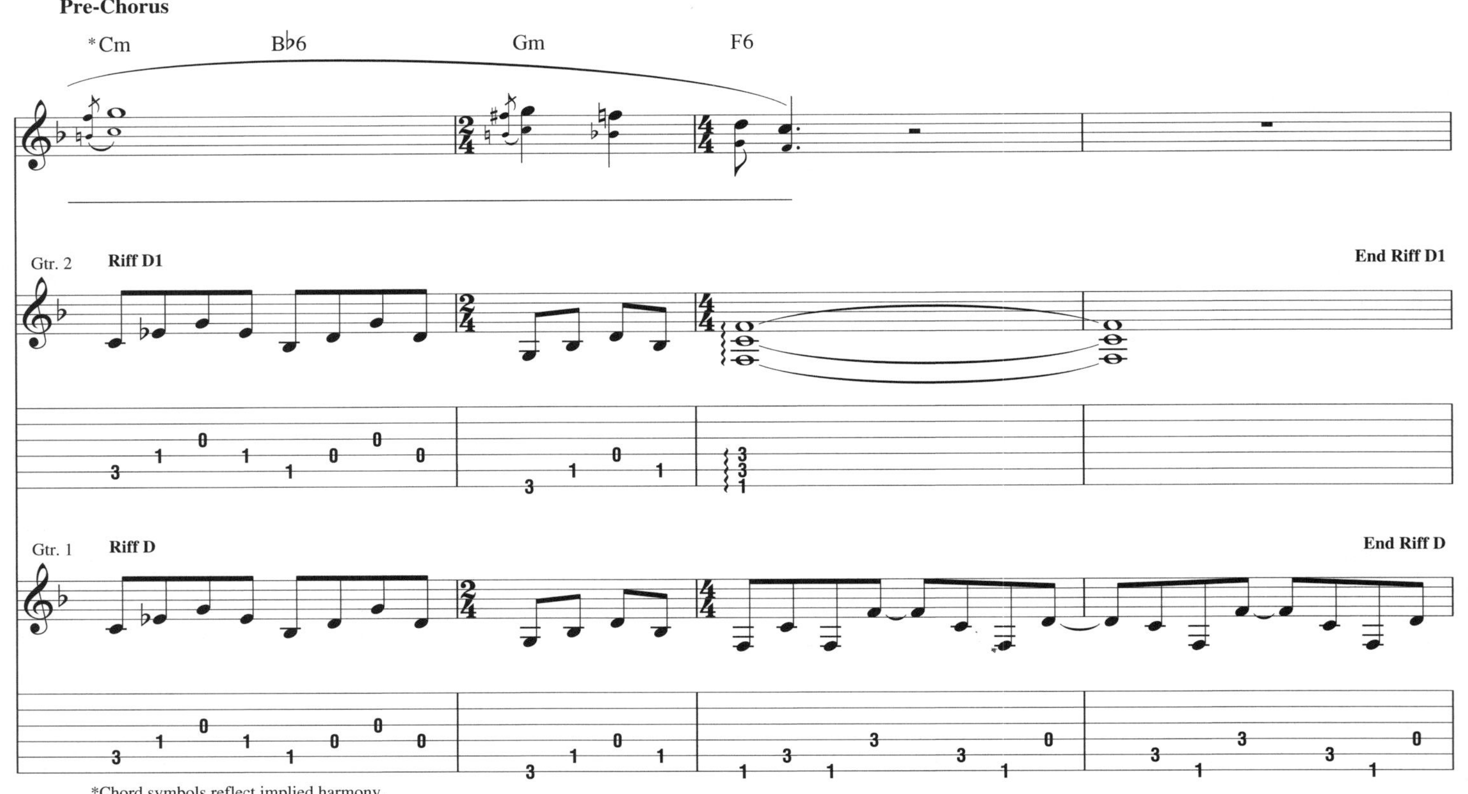

*Chord symbols reflect implied harmony.

Cm
B♭6
Gm
F6
N.C.
I am a wit - ness to your de - mise.
(cont. in slashes)
Verse
Half-time feel
Em
G
Em
G
Rhy. Fig. 3
End Rhy. Fig. 3
Gtr. 2
2. Your big - gest se - cret is one you can't keep.
Gtr. 1
Gtr. 2: w/ Rhy. Fig. 3
Em
G
Em
G
Lift up your head, if you're on - ly a - sleep.
Gtr. 1: w/ Riff C
Gtr. 2: w/ Rhy. Fig. 2 (2 times)
Em
G
You try to hold on - to rea - son. Why can't ya see that you're leav - in'?
End half-time feel
Em
G
My love for you knows no dis - tance, but it can't fight your re - sis - tance.

Pre-Chorus
Gtr. 1: w/ Riff D (2 times)
Gtr. 2: w/ Riff D1 (3 times)
Cm B♭6 Gm F6 Cm B♭6 Gm F6
I am a wit-ness to your de - mise.
Gtr. 3 (dist.)
mf
fdbk.
*Vol. swell
Pitch: G
Gtr. 3 tacet
Cm B♭6 Gm F6
I am the one who saw through the lies.
Gtrs. 4 & 5 (dist.)
Rhy. Fig. 4
End Rhy. Fig. 4
f
Gtr. 1
Chorus
Gtr. 1 tacet
2nd time, Gtrs. 6 & 7 tacet
E♭ Dm B♭ E♭ Dm B♭ Cm F
Give me the one thing you can't give.
Riff E1
Gtr. 5
Riff E
Gtr. 4

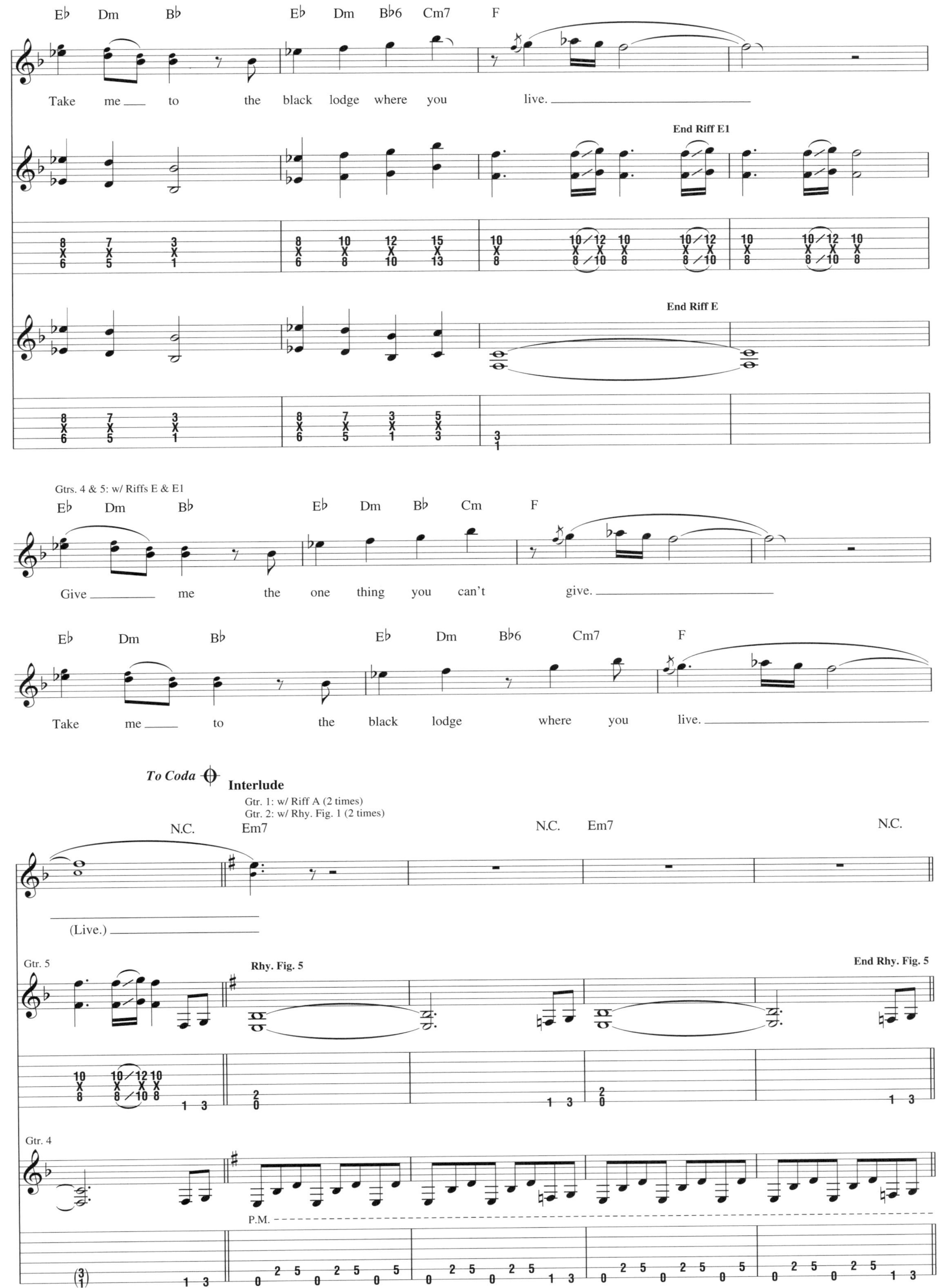

Eb Dm Bb Eb Dm Bb6 Cm7 F
Take me to the black lodge where you live.
End Riff E1
End Riff E
Gtrs. 4 & 5: w/ Riffs E & E1
Eb Dm Bb Eb Dm Bb Cm F
Give me the one thing you can't give.
Eb Dm Bb Eb Dm Bb6 Cm7 F
Take me to the black lodge where you live.
To Coda
Interlude
Gtr. 1: w/ Riff A (2 times)
Gtr. 2: w/ Rhy. Fig. 1 (2 times)
N.C. Em7 N.C. Em7 N.C.
(Live.)
Gtr. 5
Rhy. Fig. 5
End Rhy. Fig. 5
Gtr. 4
P.M.

Guitar Solo
Em7
G
N.C.
Gtr. 7 (dist.)
*Gtr. 6 (dist.)
Gtr. 3 divisi
*Played f
Gtr. 5
Rhy. Fig. 6
End Rhy. Fig. 6
P.M.
Gtr. 4
Riff F1
End Riff F1
Gtr. 1
Riff F
End Riff F
Gtrs. 1 & 4: w/ Riffs F & F1
Gtr. 5: w/ Rhy. Fig. 6

Verse
Gtr. 1: w/ Riff C
Gtr. 2: w/ Rhy. Fig. 2 (2 times)
Gtr. 3 tacet
Gtr. 4: w/ Riff F1 (1 1/4 times)
Gtr. 5: w/ Rhy. Fig. 6 (1 1/2 times)
Em
G
4. De - ny, your bod - y is scream - in'.
But your heart and your soul they're bleed - in'.
*Gtrs. 6 & 7
fdbk.
*Two gtrs. arr. for one.
Em
Gtrs. 6 & 7 tacet
G5
Gtr. 5
(cont. in notation)
Just to fall a - sleep is a god - send,
un - til your de - mons ap - pear a - gain.
Gtr. 6
Gtr. 4
P.M.
Pre-Chorus
Cm
B♭
Gm
F
Gtr. 7
fdbk.
Gtr. 6
Pitch: G
Gtrs. 4 & 5
Rhy. Fig. 7
End Rhy. Fig. 7
P.M.

Gtrs. 4 & 5: w/ Rhy. Fig. 7 (2 times)
Cm
B♭
Gm
F
I am a wit - ness to your de - mise.
Gtr. 7
Gtr. 6
Cm
B♭
Gm
F
I am the one who saw through the lies.
P.M.
P.M.
P.M.
D.S. al Coda
Gtrs. 4 & 5: w/ Rhy. Fig. 7 (1st 2 meas.)
Gtrs. 4 & 5: w/ Rhy. Fig. 4
Cm
B♭
Gm
F
My love has al - ways been blind.
P.M.
P.M.
P.M.

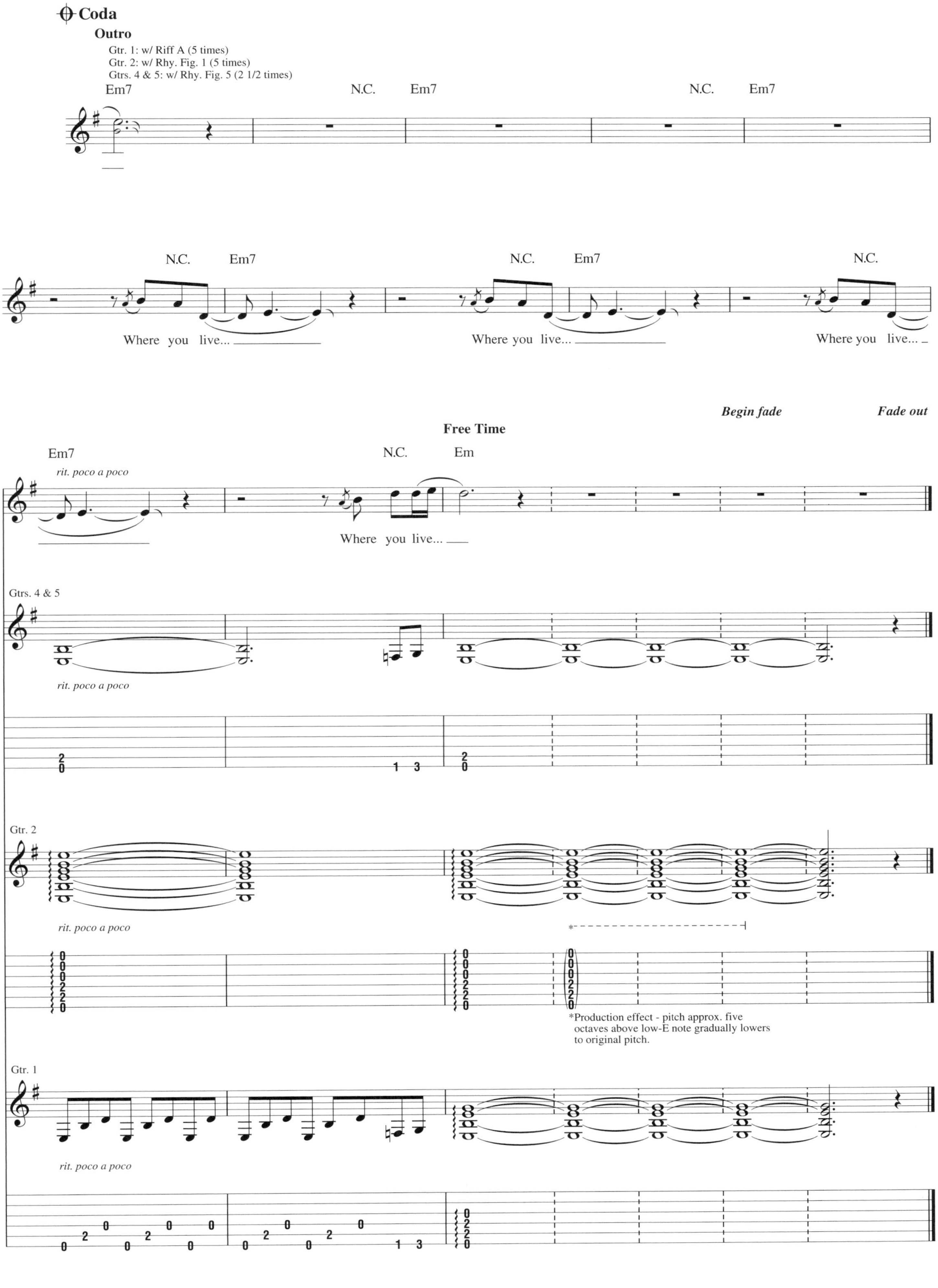

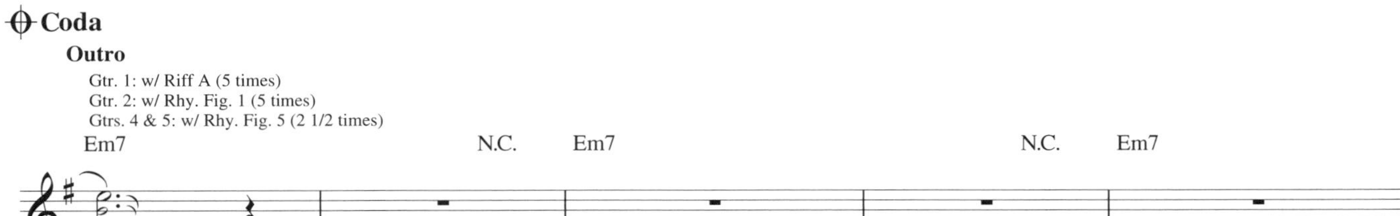

Free Time

Begin fade

Fade out

Em7 N.C. Em

rit. poco a poco

Where you live...

Gtrs. 4 & 5

rit. poco a poco

Gtr. 2

rit. poco a poco

*Production effect - pitch approx. five octaves above low-E note gradually lowers to original pitch.

Gtr. 1

rit. poco a poco

from *Attack of the Killer B's*

Bring the Noise

Words and Music by Joseph Bellardini, Frank Bello, Charlie Benante, Scott Rosenfeld, Daniel Spitz, Carlton Ridenhour, James Boxley III and Eric Sadler

Tune down 1/2 step:
(low to high) E♭-A♭-D♭-G♭-B♭-E♭

*Doubled throughout

**Chord symbols reflect implied harmony.

F5 E5 B♭5 E5 F5 E5 B♭5 E5
Once a - gain, back is the in - cred - i - ble rhyme an - i - mal, the young can - ni - bal.
he can cut a rec - ord from side to side. So what? The ride, the glide should be much saf - er than a su - i - cide.
End Rhy. Fig. 1
P.M.
Gtr. 1: w/ Rhy. Fig. 1 (3 times)
F5 E5 B♭5 E5 F5 E5 B♭5 E5
D! Pub - lic en - e - my num - ber one. Five - O said, "Freeze!" and I got numb.
Soul con - trol, beat is the fa - ther of your rock 'n' roll. Mu - sic for what-cha, for which - in' you call a band, man.
F5 E5 B♭5 E5 F5 E5 B♭5 E5
Can't I tell 'em that I real - ly nev - er had a gun? But it's the wax that the Ter - mi - na - tor X spun.
Mak - in' a mu - sic, a - buse it, but you can't do it, you know. You call 'em dem - os, but we ride lim - os, too.
2nd time, Gtr. 1: w/ Rhy. Fig. 1 (2 times)
F5 E5 B♭5 E5 F5 E5 B♭5 E5
Now they got me in a cell 'cause my rec - ords they sell 'cause a broth - er like me said, "Well,
Lis - ten for les - sons I'm say - in' in - side mu - sic that the crit - ics all are blast - in' me for.
What - cha gon - na do? Rap is not a - fraid of you. Beat is for Son - ny Bo - no, beat is for Yo - ko O - no.
F5 E5 B♭5 E5 F5 E5 B♭5 E5
Far - ra - khan's a proph - et and I think you ought to lis - ten to what he can say to you." What you ought to do is
They'll nev - er care for the broth - ers and sis - ters a - cross the coun - try has us up for the war.
Run D M C first said a D. J. could be a band, stand on it's own feet, got you out your seat.
F5 E5 B♭5 E5 F5 E5 B♭5 E5
fol - low for now. pow - er to the peo - ple. Say, "Make a mir - a - cle. D, pump the lyr - i - cal."
We got to dem - on - strate. Come on, now. They're gon - na have to wait 'til we got it right.
Beat is for Er - ic B. and L.L. as well. Hell, wax is for An - thrax, still it can rock bells.
F5 E5 B♭5 E5 F5 E5 B♭5 E5
Black is back, all in, we're gon - na win. Check it out. Here we go a - gain.
Yeah, y'all. Come on!
Ra - di - o sta - tions, I ques - tion their black - ness. They call them - selves black, but we'll see if they'll play this.
Ev - er for - ev - er, u - ni - ver - sal, it will sell. Time for me to ex - it, Ter - mi - na - tor X it.

Chorus
G5 B♭5 G5 B♭5 G5
B♭5 G5 B♭5 G5
Turn it up!
Bring the noise!
Rhy. Fig. 2
End Rhy. Fig. 2
Gtr. 1
P.M.
*Gang vocals, next 6 meas.
Gtr. 1: w/ Rhy. Fig. 2 (3 times)
B♭5 G5 B♭5 G5
B♭5 G5 B♭5 G5
G5 B♭5 G5 B♭5 G5
Turn it up!
To Coda 1
To Coda 2
B♭5 G5 B♭5 G5
B♭5 G5 B♭5 G5
B♭5 G5 B♭5 G5
Bring the noise!
2. Nev - er
Verse
E5 N.C.
Gtr. 1 tacet
bad - der than bad 'cause the broth - er is mad - der than mad at the fact that's cor - rupt like a sen - a - tor.
Gtr. 1
D.S. al Coda 1
Soul on a roll. Would you treat it like soap on a rope 'cause the beats and the lines are so dope?
Coda 1
D.S.S. al Coda 2
B♭5 G5 B♭5 G5
B♭5 G5 B♭5 G5
3. Get
Coda 2
B♭5 G5 B♭5 G5
B♭5 G5 B♭5 G5

Bridge
E5 G5 A5 E5 G5 A5
Do, do, do, do, do, do. Do, do, do, do, do, do.
Gtr. 1
Rhy. Fig. 3
End Rhy. Fig. 3
P.M.
w/ misc. vocals
Gtr. 1: w/ Rhy. Fig. 3 (2 times)
4. From
Verse
Gtr. 1: w/ Rhy. Fig. 1 (3 times)
F5 E5 B♭5 E5
coast to coast so you stop be - in' like a co - ma - tose. Stan, my man, the beat's the same when I boast those.
Rock with some piz - zazz. It will last. Why you ask? Roll with the rock stars.
You nev - er get ac - cept - ed as.
We got to plead the fifth, we can't in - ves - ti - gate. Don't need to wait, get the rec - ord straight. Hey!
Pos - se in ef - fect got fla - vor Ter - mi - na - tor X to sign checks, play - in' to get paid.
We got to check it out down on the av - e - nue, a mag - a - zine or two is dis - sin' me or dis - sin' you.
Yeah, I'm tell - in' you.

Outro
w/ misc. vocals
Gtr. 1: w/ Riff A
E5
Gtr. 2 (dist.)
f
Spoken: Yo, check out this beat.
B♭5
E5
N.C.
Gtr. 2
P.M.
Gtr. 1
P.M.
P.M.
P.M.
w/ misc. vocals
Gtrs. 1 & 2 tacet
(Drums)
(Sampled drum loop)
Sample: Hear the drum-mer get wick - ed. Hear the drum-mer get
wick - ed. Hear the drum - mer get wick - ed. Hear the drum - mer get
wick - ed. H - h - h - h - hear the... H - h - h - h -
hear the dru', hear the dru', hear the drum - mer get wick - ed.

from *Among the Living*

Caught in a Mosh

Words and Music by Joseph Bellardini, Frank Bello, Charlie Benante, Scott Rosenfeld and Daniel Spitz

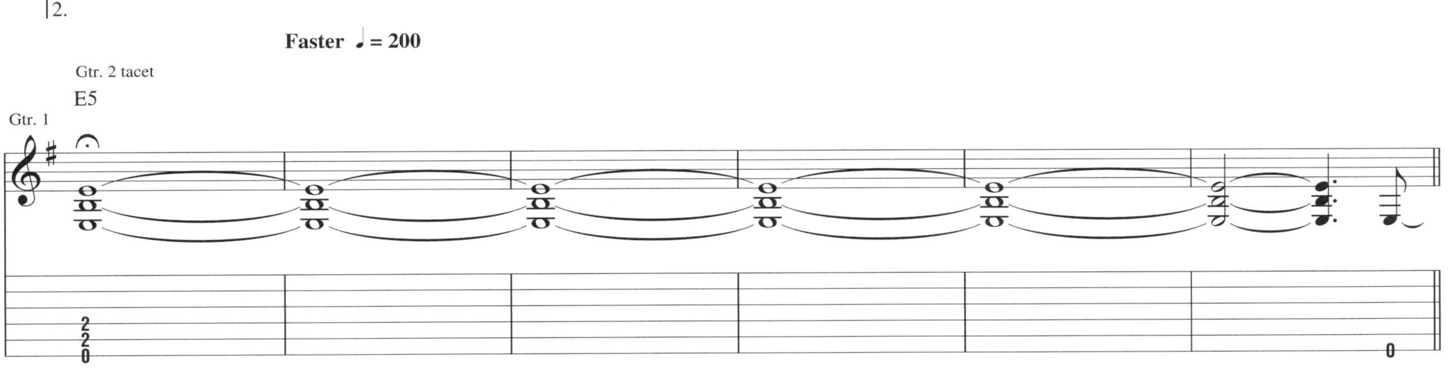

3.
Faster ♩ = 224
N.C.
Verse
E5
B5 C5 E5 F5 E5 D♯5 E5
Yelled:
1. Why don't you lis-ten when I try to talk to you?
Stop
Rhy. Fig. 1
P.M.
think-ing of your-self for just a sec-ond, fool.
Shut up, shut up. I don't want to hear your mouth.
Your

B5 C5 E5 F5 E5 D♯5 E5 G5 F♯5
moth-er made a mon - ster. Now get the hell out of my house.
End Rhy. Fig. 1
P.M.
Pre-Chorus
Slower ♩ = 208
E5 F♯5 E5 F5 E5 F♯5 E5 F5 E5 F♯5 G5 F♯5
Can't stand it for an - oth - er day.
Yelled: (I ain't gon-na live my life this way.
Riff B
End Riff B
Cold sweat, my fists are clench - ing. The id - i - ot con-ven-tion.
Stomp, stomp, stomp.)
Chorus
D5 F5 C5 E5
Which one of these words don't you un - der - stand?
Rhy. Fig. 2
End Rhy. Fig. 2

Yelled: All caught in a mosh.
0 0 1 0 0 3 0 0
4 0 5 0 6 7 8 0
0 1 0 0 3 0 0
4 0 5 0 8 7 6 5

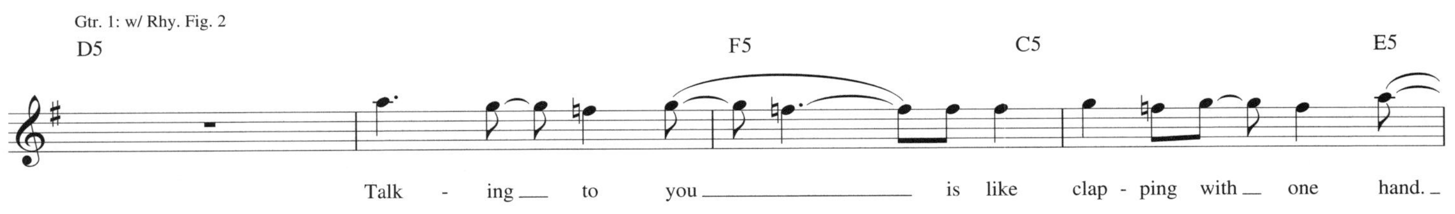
Gtr. 1: w/ Rhy. Fig. 2
D5
F5
C5
E5
Talk - ing to you is like clap - ping with one hand.

Yelled: (Caught in a mosh. Caught in a
Yelled: (What is it? What is it?
Gtr. 1
Riff C
End Riff C
0 0 1 0 0 3 0 0
4 0 5 0 6 7 8 0
0 1 0 0 3 0 0
4 0 5 0 8 7 6 0

To Coda 1
To Coda 2
mosh. Caught in a mosh. Caught in a
What is it? What is it?)
(0) 0 1 0 0 3 0 0
4 0 5 0 6 7 8 0
0 1 0 0 3 0 0
4 0 5 0 8 7 6

Verse
Faster ♩ = 216
Gtr. 1: w/ Rhy. Fig. 1
E5
B5 C5 E5 F5 E5 D♯5 E5
2. Don't tell me how to do my job.
mosh.)
Yelled: There's the door, your name's on the knob.
You're
al - ways in the way like a beast on my back.
Were you
D.S. al Coda 1
G5 F♯5
dropped as a ba - by? 'Cause brains you lack.
Coda 1
Slower ♩ = 169
Caught in a mosh.)
Screamed: Ah.
Interlude
E5 C5 F♯5 G5 E5 A5 B5
Rhy. Fig. 3
End Rhy. Fig. 3
P.M.

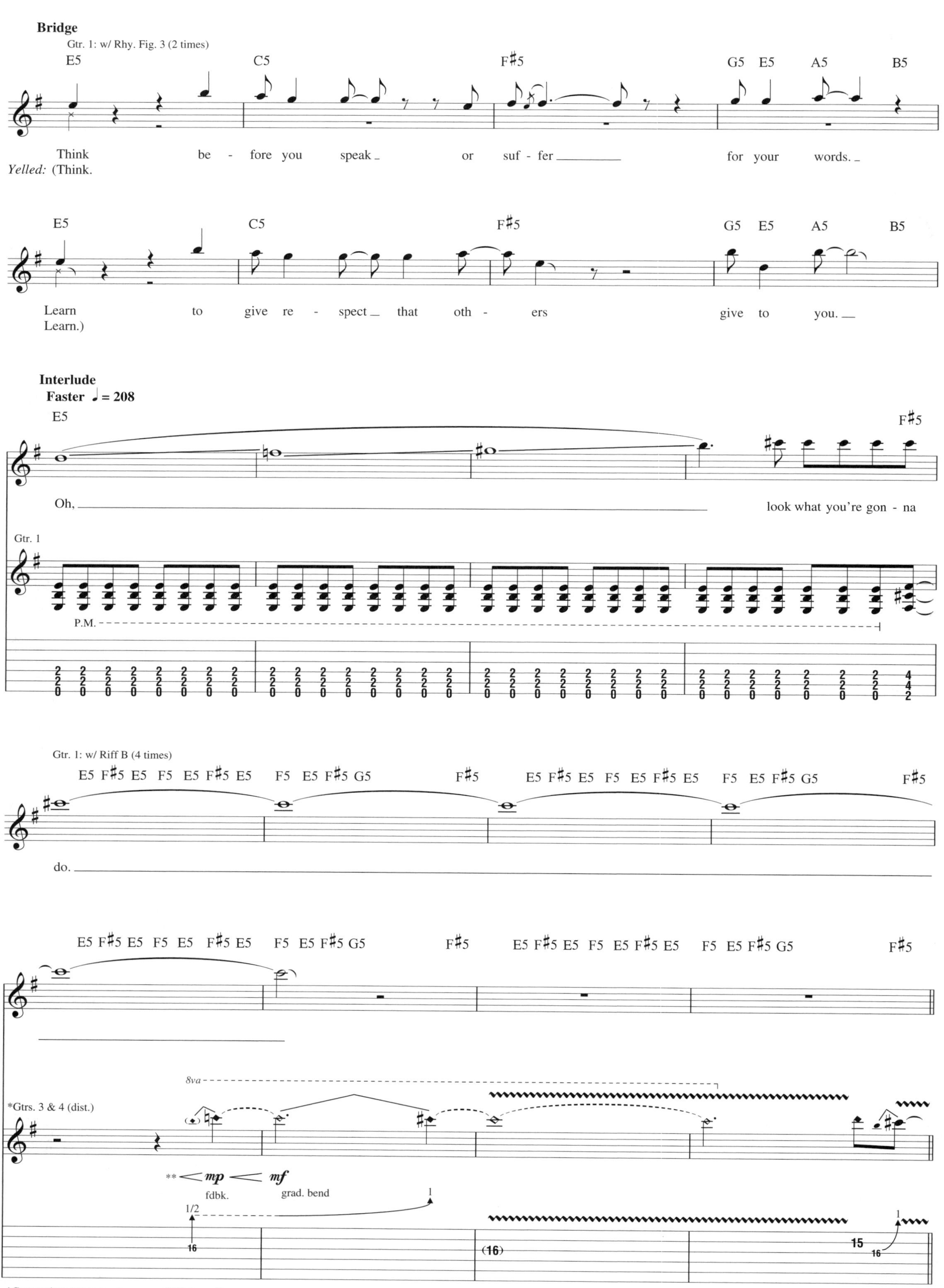
Bridge
Gtr. 1: w/ Rhy. Fig. 3 (2 times)
E5
C5
F♯5
G5 E5 A5 B5
Think be - fore you speak _ or suf - fer _ for your words. _
Yelled: (Think.
E5
C5
F♯5
G5 E5 A5 B5
Learn to give re - spect _ that oth - ers give to you. _
Learn.)
Interlude
Faster ♩ = 208
E5
F♯5
Oh, _ look what you're gon - na
Gtr. 1
P.M.
Gtr. 1: w/ Riff B (4 times)
E5 F♯5 E5 F5 E5 F♯5 E5 F5 E5 F♯5 G5 F♯5 E5 F♯5 E5 F5 E5 F♯5 E5 F5 E5 F♯5 G5 F♯5
do. _
E5 F♯5 E5 F5 E5 F♯5 E5 F5 E5 F♯5 G5 F♯5 E5 F♯5 E5 F5 E5 F♯5 E5 F5 E5 F♯5 G5 F♯5
8va
*Gtrs. 3 & 4 (dist.)
** mp mf
fdbk.
grad. bend
1/2
1
1
*Composite arrangement
**Vol. swell

Guitar Solo

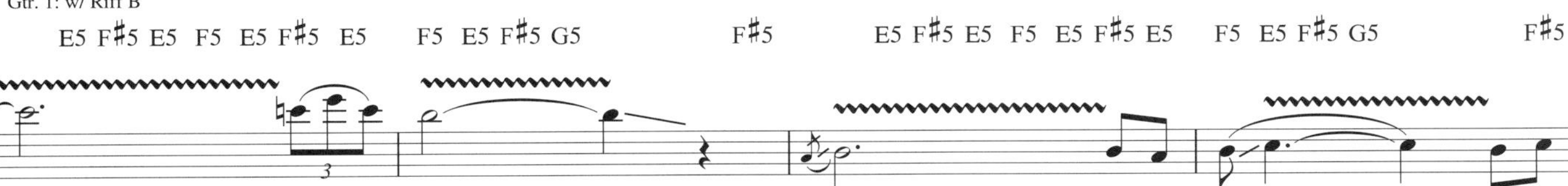
Gtr. 1: w/ Riff B
E5 F#5 E5 F5 E5 F#5 E5
F5 E5 F#5 G5
F#5
E5 F#5 E5 F5 E5 F#5 E5
F5 E5 F#5 G5
F#5

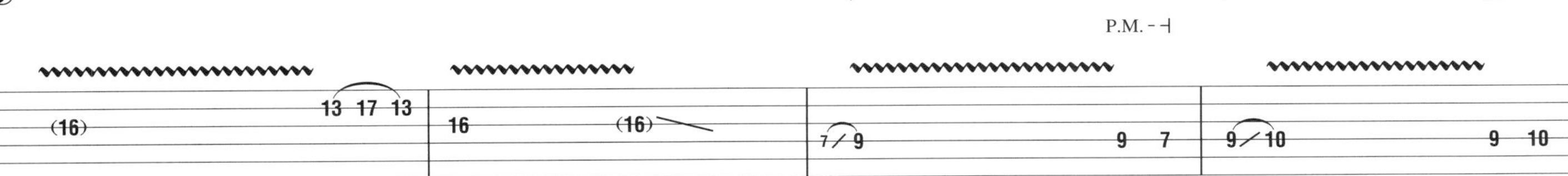
P.M.

E5 F#5 E5 F5 E5 F#5 E5
F5 E5 F#5 G5
F#5
E5 F#5 E5 F5 E5 F#5 E5
F5 E5 F#5 G5
E5
Gtrs. 3 & 4
P.M.
Gtr. 1
P.M.
P.M.

G5 E5 G5 E5
G5 E5 G5 E5
F#5
E5
G5 E5 G5 E5
G5 E5 G5 E5
B5
Gtrs. 3 & 4
Gtr. 1
P.M.
P.M.
P.M.
P.M.
P.M.
P.M.
P.M.
P.M.
P.M.
P.M.

E5 G5 E5 G5 E5 G5 E5 G5 E5 F#5 E5 G5 E5 G5 E5 G5 E5 G5 E5 B5
Gtr. 3
P.M.
P.M.
w/ bar
slack
Gtr. 4
P.M.
P.M.
w/ bar
grad. dive
slack
Gtr. 1
P.M.
Interlude
E5 C5 E5
Riff D
*Gtrs. 3 & 4
grad. bend
*Composite arrangement
Gtr. 5 (dist.)
Riff E
mf
grad. bend
Rhy. Fig. 4
Gtr. 1
P.M.

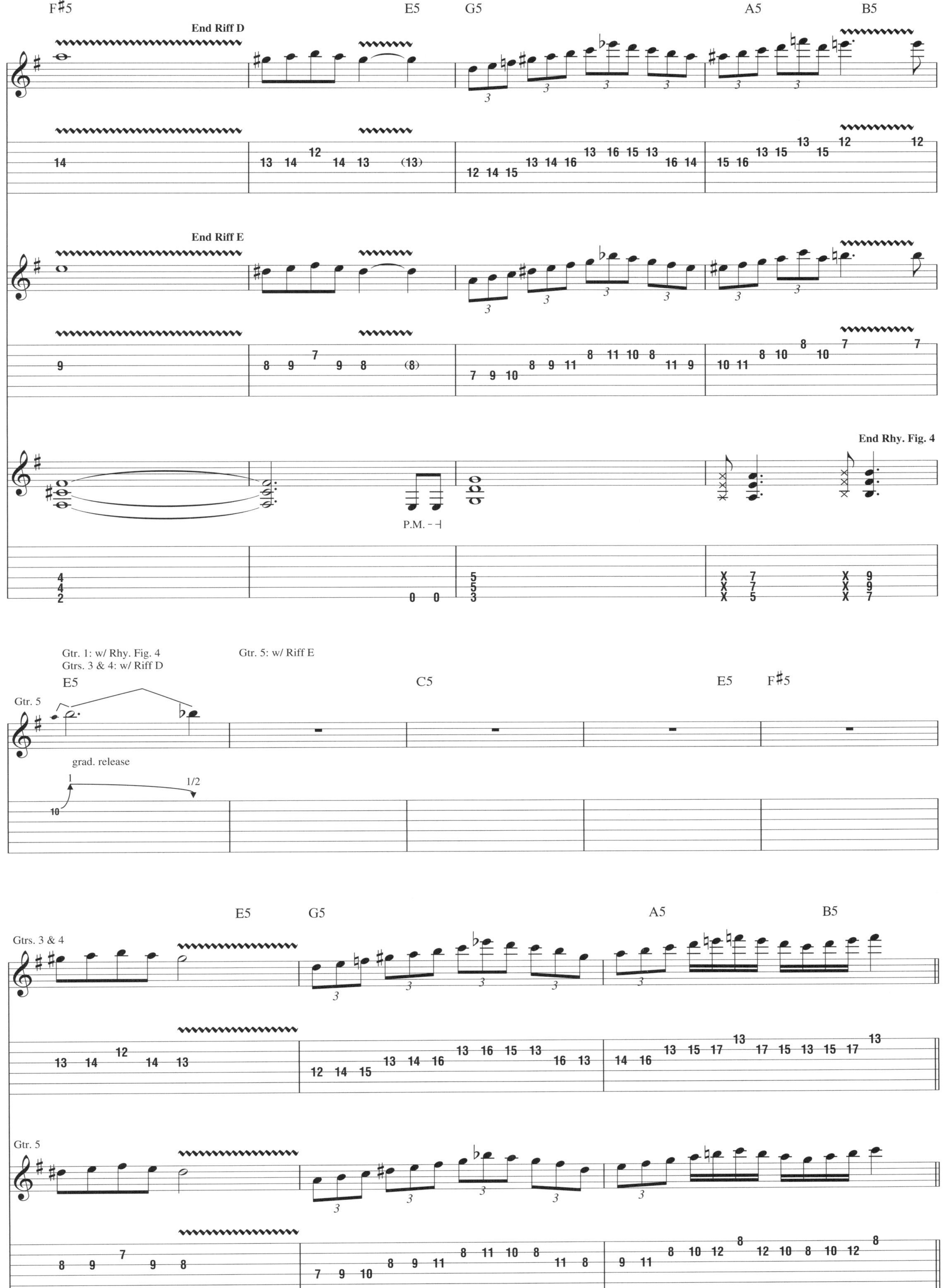
F♯5
End Riff D
E5
G5
A5
B5
End Riff E
End Rhy. Fig. 4
P.M.
Gtr. 1: w/ Rhy. Fig. 4
Gtrs. 3 & 4: w/ Riff D
Gtr. 5: w/ Riff E
E5
C5
E5
F♯5
Gtr. 5
grad. release
1
1/2
E5
G5
A5
B5
Gtrs. 3 & 4
Gtr. 5

Interlude

Gtr. 1: w/ Riff C

Gtr. 5 tacet

E5

Gtr. 3

8va

1/2 3/4 1

17 (17) 20 22 (22) 22

Gtr. 4

8va

1/2 1

17 (17) 20 22 (22) 22

Gtr. 5

12 (12) 15

Gtr. 1: w/ Riff A (2 times)

Gtrs. 3 & 4 tacet

Gtr. 3

8va

(22) (22)

Gtr. 4

8va

(22) (22)

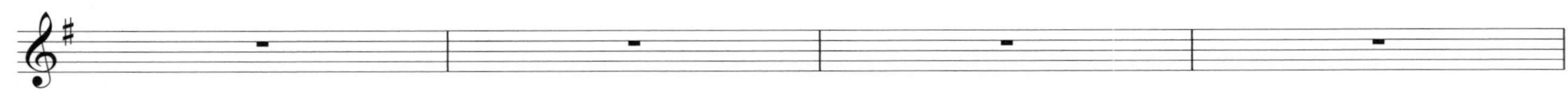

3. Yelled: Hey,
Gtr. 1
Verse
B5 C5 E5 F5 E5 D♯5 E5
man,
I'm
P.M.
Gtr. 1: w/ Rhy. Fig. 1 (last 12 meas.)
E5
try - ing to rea - son but you don't un - der - stand.
Talk - ing in cir - cles we'll nev - er get it straight.
Just
D.S. al Coda 2
G5 F♯5
you and me and our the - a - tre of hate.
Coda 2
Free time
N.C. G5 E5 A♯5 B5 C5 E5 C5
Caught in a mosh.)

from *Persistence of Time*

Got the Time

Words and Music by Joe Jackson

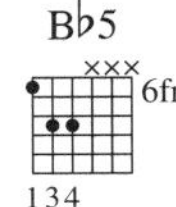

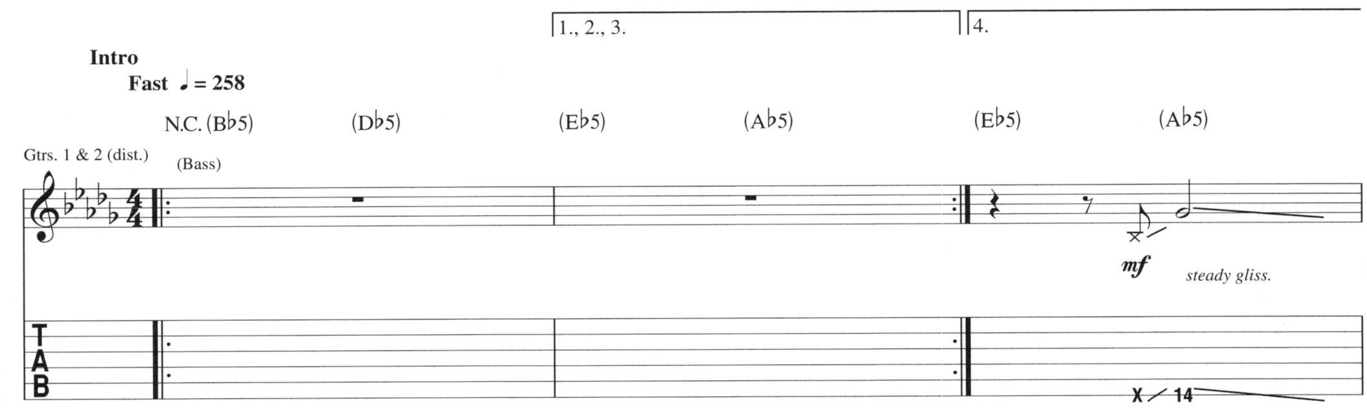

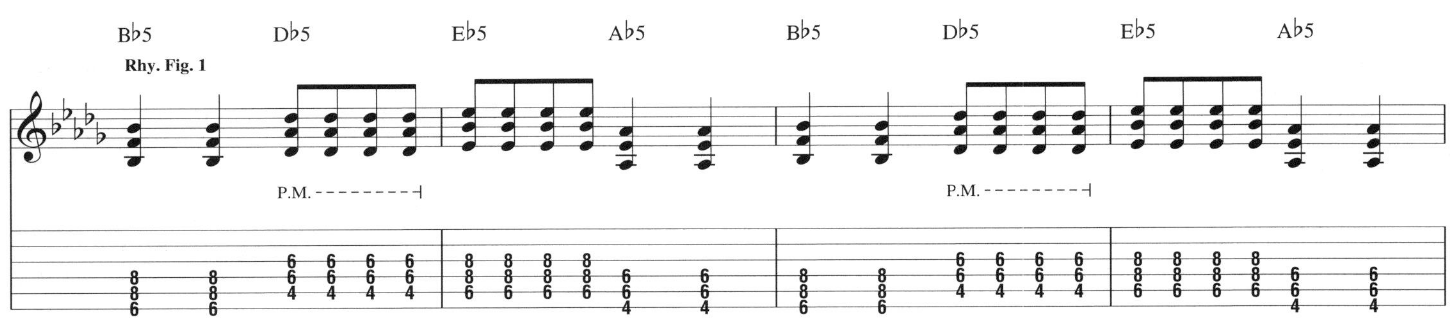

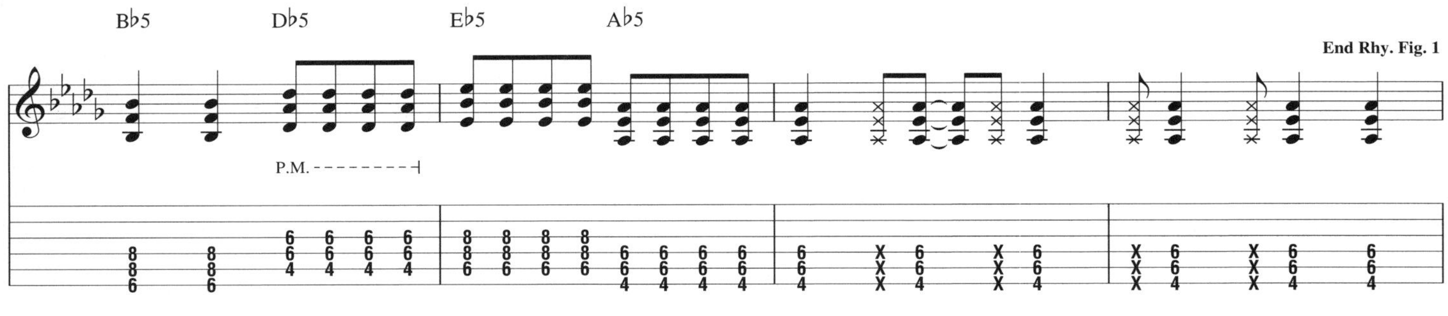

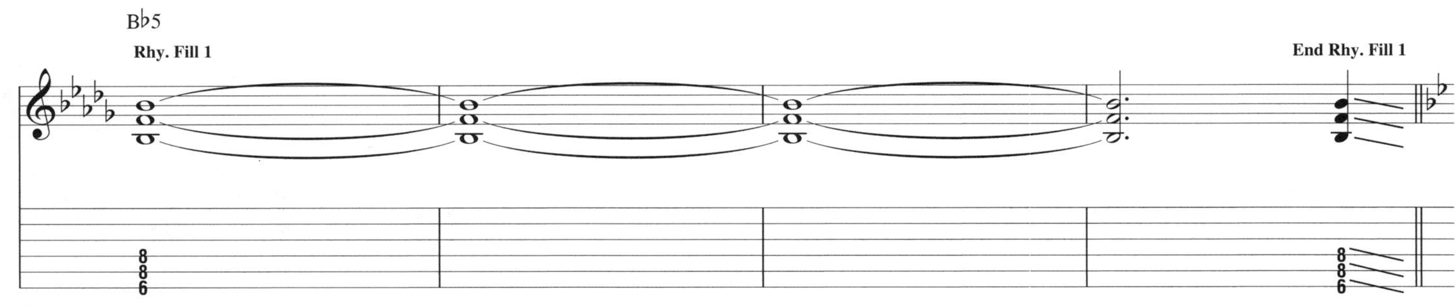

Verse
B♭5
N.C.
1. Wake up, got an-oth-er day to get. Through now, got an-oth-er man to see.
2. If I tell you what I'm do-ing to-day will you shut up and get out of my
Rhy. Fill 2
End Rhy. Fill 2
B♭5
Got-ta call him on the tel-e-phone. Way, oh, got-ta find a piece of pa-per.
way. Some-one ask me what the time is, I don't know, on-ly know I got-ta go now.
P.M.
P.M.
Gtrs. 1 & 2: w/ Rhy. Fill 2
N.C.
Sit down, got an-oth-er let-ter to write. Think hard, got to get the let-ter just right.
No time, try to get my watch re-paired. No time, nev-er got a thing to wear.
B♭5
A♭5
Hear the ring-ing on the tel-e-phone. Whoa, no, got-ta write an-oth-er let-ter.
hear it ring-ing in my head now.
Gtrs. 1 & 2
P.M.
P.M.

Pre-Chorus
Gb5
F5
Db5
Eb5
N.C.
No such thing as to - mor - row. All we want.
(All we want. Two, three, go.)
Chorus
1st & 2nd times, Gtrs. 1 & 2: w/ Rhy. Fig. 1 (2 times)
3rd time, Gtrs. 1 & 2: w/ Rhy. Fig. 1 (2 1/2 times)
Bb5
Db5
Eb5
Ab5
Time. Got the time tick, tick, tick-ing in my head. Got the time tick, tick, tick-ing in my head. Got the time
(Time. Time. Time.)
To Coda 2
tick, tick, tick-ing in my head, tick-ing in my head, tick-ing in my
head, tick-ing in my head.
To Coda 1
Interlude
Gtrs. 1 & 2: w/ Rhy. Fill 1
D.S. al Coda 1
Coda 1
Interlude
Gtr. 3 (dist.)
mf
Gtrs. 1 & 2
P.M.

B♭5
D♭5
E♭5
A♭5
P.M.
Bass Solo
Gtr. 3 tacet
B♭5
Gtrs. 1 & 2
(Gtr. 2, cont. in slashes)
B♭5
8va
Gtr. 1
fdbk.
Pitch: C
8va
8va
(cont. in notation)

Gtrs. 1 & 2
loco
1.
2.
D.S.S. al Coda 2
Ab5
P.M.
Coda 2
Bb5 Db5 Eb5 Ab5
head. Got the time tick, tick, tick-ing in my head. Got the time tick, tick, tick-ing in my
(Time Time.
head. Got the time tick, tick, tick-ing in my head, tick-ing in my
Time.)
head, tick-ing in my head, tick-ing in my
head. ___
N.C.
Gtrs. 1 & 2
P.M.

from *Attack of the Killer B's*

I'm the Man '91

Words and Music by Joseph Bellardini, Frank Bello, Charlie Benante, Scott Rosenfeld, Daniel Spitz and John Rooney

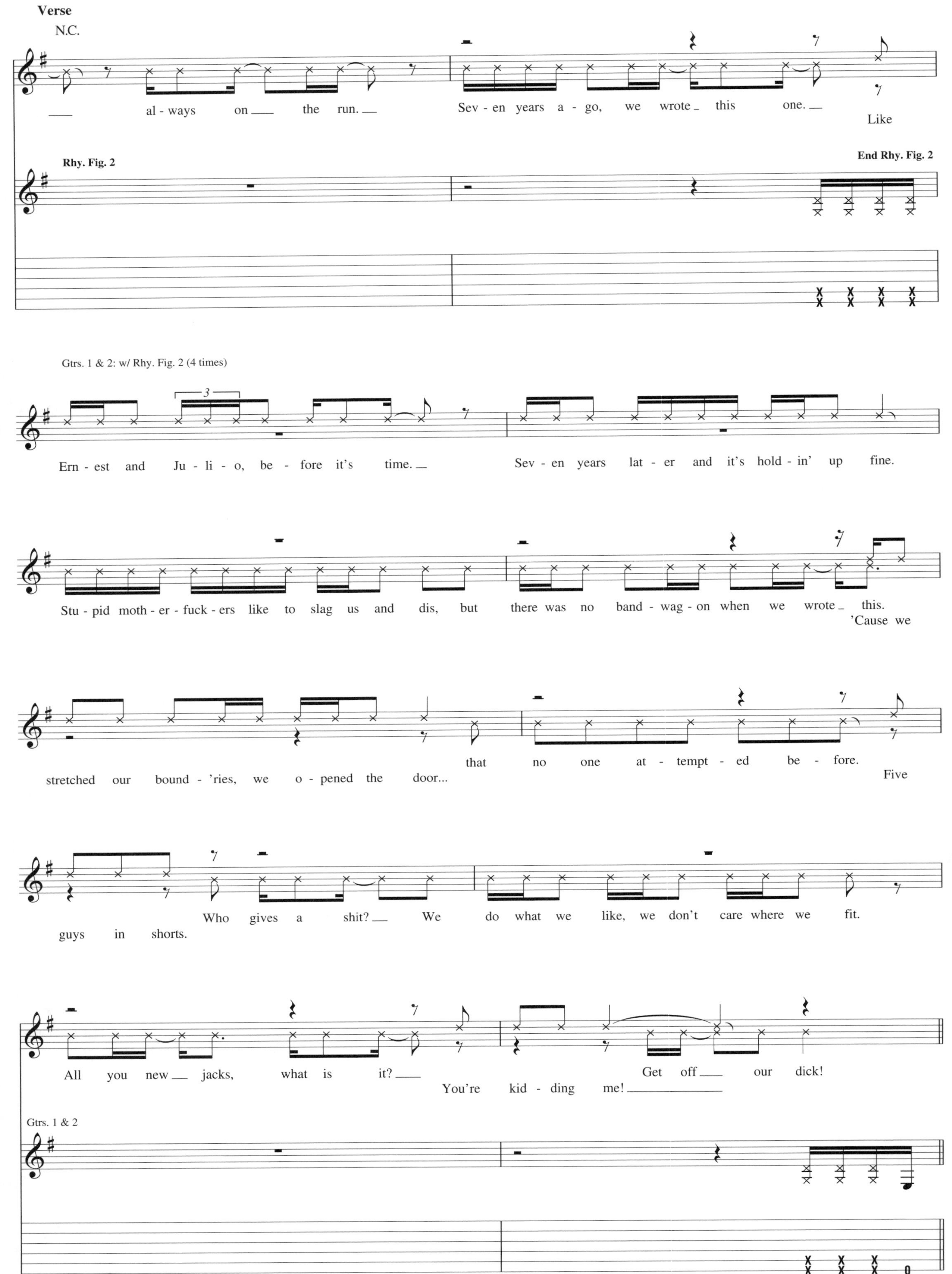
Verse
N.C.
always on the run.
Seven years ago, we wrote this one.
Like
Rhy. Fig. 2
End Rhy. Fig. 2
Gtrs. 1 & 2: w/ Rhy. Fig. 2 (4 times)
Ernest and Julio, before it's time.
Seven years later and it's holdin' up fine.
Stupid motherfuckers like to slag us and dis, but
there was no bandwagon when we wrote this.
'Cause we
stretched our bound-'ries, we opened the door...
that no one attempted before.
Five
guys in shorts.
Who gives a shit? We
do what we like, we don't care where we fit.
All you new jacks, what is it?
You're kidding me!
Get off our dick!
Gtrs. 1 & 2

Interlude
G5
B5 A5 G5
B5
D5 C5 B5
C5
E♭5 D5 C5
B5
A5 G♯5 A5 B5
Rhy. Fig. 3
P.M.
N.C.
2. Now, we're
End Rhy. Fig. 3
Verse
E5
F5
E♭5
An - thrax... and we take no shit. And we don't care for writ - ing hits. The
Rhy. Fig. 4
sound you hear is what we like. And I'll steal your Pop - Tarts like I stole your... Ah, ah,
End Rhy. Fig. 4

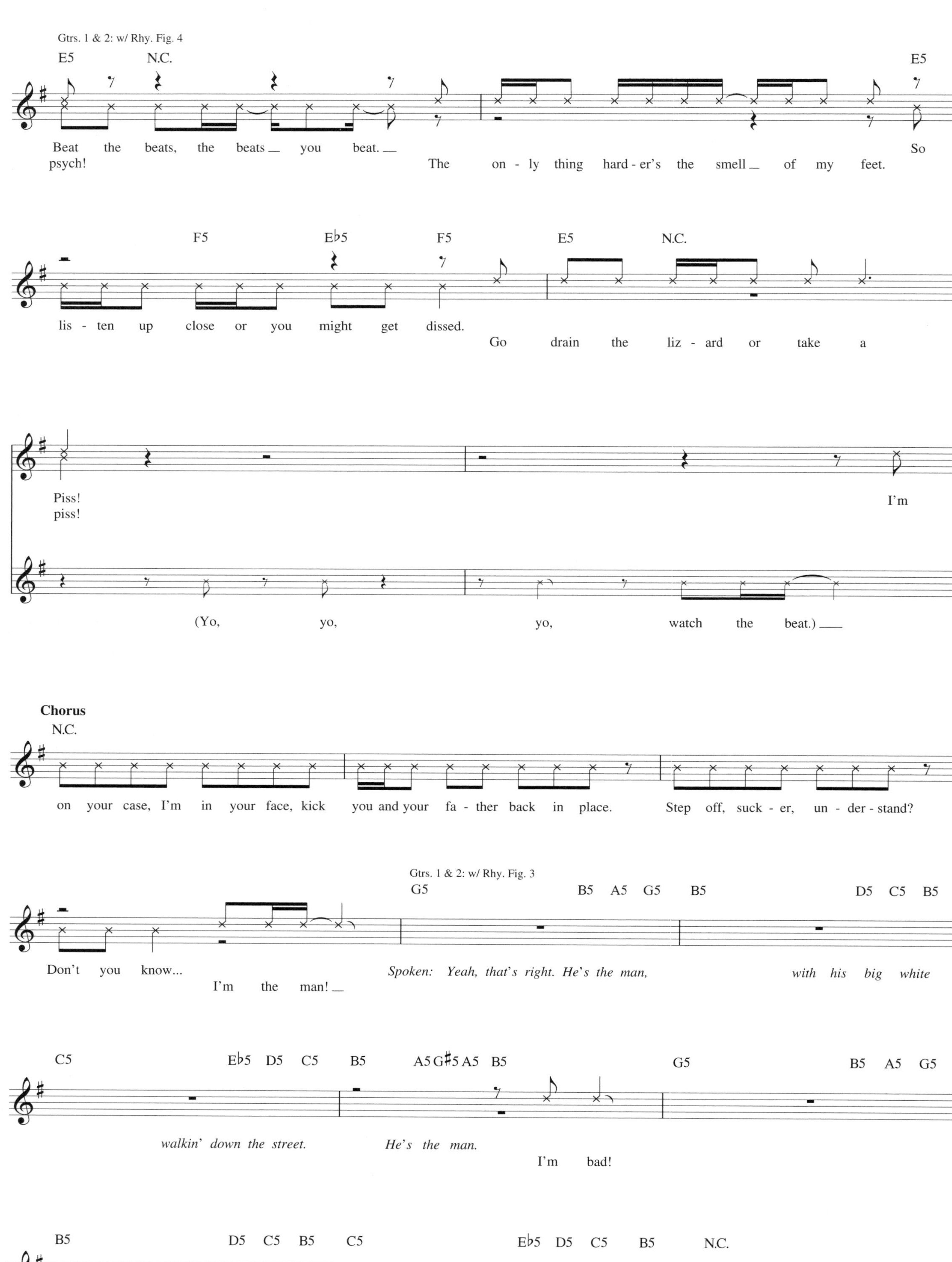

Gtrs. 1 & 2: w/ Rhy. Fig. 4
E5
N.C.
E5
Beat the beats, the beats you beat.
So
psych!
The only thing hard-er's the smell of my feet.
F5
E♭5
F5
E5
N.C.
lis-ten up close or you might get dissed.
Go drain the liz-ard or take a
Piss!
I'm
piss!
(Yo, yo, yo, watch the beat.)
Chorus
N.C.
on your case, I'm in your face, kick you and your fa-ther back in place. Step off, suck-er, un-der-stand?
Gtrs. 1 & 2: w/ Rhy. Fig. 3
G5
B5 A5 G5
B5
D5 C5 B5
Don't you know...
I'm the man!
Spoken: Yeah, that's right. He's the man,
with his big white
C5
E♭5 D5 C5
B5
A5 G♯5 A5 B5
G5
B5 A5 G5
walkin' down the street.
He's the man.
I'm bad!
B5
D5 C5 B5
C5
E♭5 D5 C5
B5
N.C.
Huh!
3. We got

Verse
E5
N.C.
E5
real def rhy-thms, fresh new jams. E-gos! Scott!
And fresh new jams. If you think we got e-goes, well, we're just hams. Scott
Gtrs. 1 & 2
P.M.
F5
E♭5
F5
E5
N.C.
Frank-ie's nev-er on time, he's al - ways...
plays stick - ball, likes to skate. Late.
P.M.
Gtrs. 1 & 2: w/ Rhy. Fig. 1
G5
N.C.
Drink-in' these drinks, the drinks I drank.
I put my mon-ey in the bank. They
E5
F5
E♭5
F5
E5
N.C.
cut their crack, they of - fer joints.
We don't do drugs. Do you get our
Gtrs. 1 & 2
P.M.

Gtrs. 1 & 2 tacet
mean - ing?
(Point, point, point, point. And watch the beat.)
I'm
Chorus
N.C.
on your case, I'm in your face, kick you and your fa - ther back in place.
Step off, suck - er, un - der - stand? Don't you know...
I'm the man!
G5 B5 A5 G5 B5 D5 C5 B5 C5 E♭5 D5 C5 E5
Spoken: That's right. He's the man. That's right. That's right. He's bad!
I'm bad!
I'm the man!
Gtrs. 1 & 2
P.M.
Gtrs. 1 & 2: w/ Rhy. Fig. 3 (last 4 meas.)
G5 B5 A5 G5 B5 D5 C5 B5 C5 E♭5 D5 C5 E5 N.C.
4. Oh, for a
Verse
E5
heav - y met - al band, rap's a dif - f'rent way.
We like to be dif - f'rent and not cli - ché.
Well, they
Rhy. Fig. 5
End Rhy. Fig. 5
Gtrs. 1 & 2
P.M.

F5
Eb5
F5
E5
N.C.
say rap and met - al can nev - er mix.
Well, all of them can suck our
P.M.
P.M.
P.M.
Gtrs. 1 & 2: w/ Rhy. Fig. 5
E5
Fart the farts, the farts he fart - ed.
dicks. I pick my fuck - in' nose, but I'm not re - tard - ed.
Like El
F5
Eb5
F5
E5
N.C.
Du - ce says, "Smell my an - al vap - or."
And wipe my butt...
with your fuck - in'
Gtrs. 1 & 2
P.M.
P.M.
P.M.
Gtrs. 1 & 2 tacet
face.
(You stu - pid id - i - ot.)
I'm
Chorus
N.C.
on your case, I'm in your face, kick you and your fa - ther back in place. Step off, suck - er, un - der - stand?
Gtrs. 1 & 2: w/ Rhy. Fig. 3 (1st 5 meas.)
G5
B5
A5
G5
B5
D5
C5
B5
Don't you know...
Spoken: That's right. You're listening to the man.
I'm the man!
I'm bad!

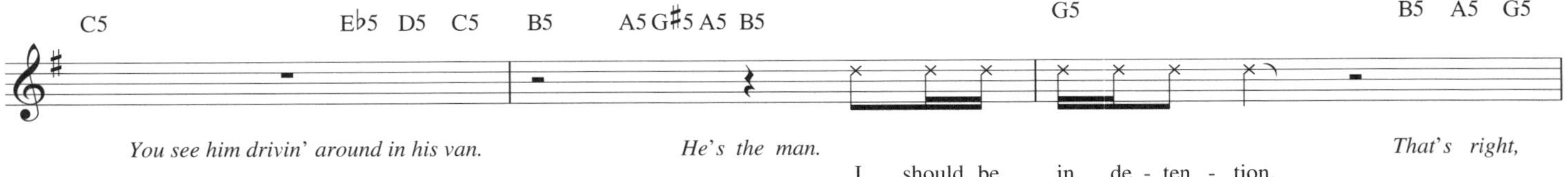
C5
E♭5 D5 C5
B5
A5 G♯5 A5 B5
G5
B5 A5 G5
You see him drivin' around in his van.
He's the man.
That's right,
I should be in de - ten - tion.

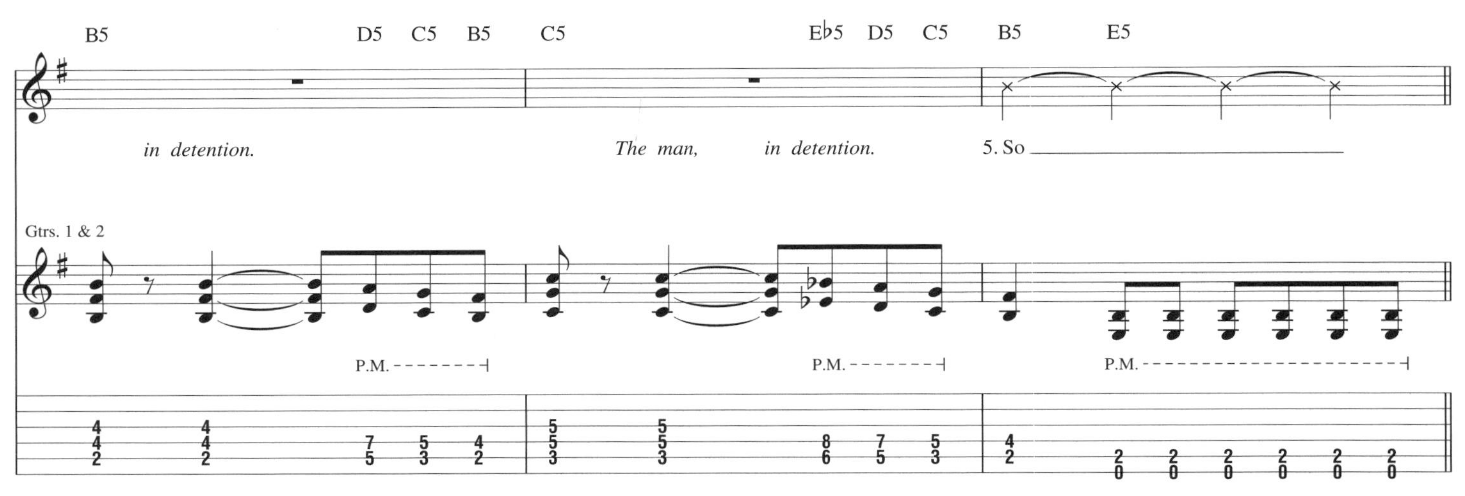
B5
D5 C5 B5
C5
E♭5 D5 C5
B5
E5
in detention.
The man, in detention.
5. So
Gtrs. 1 & 2
P.M.
P.M.
P.M.

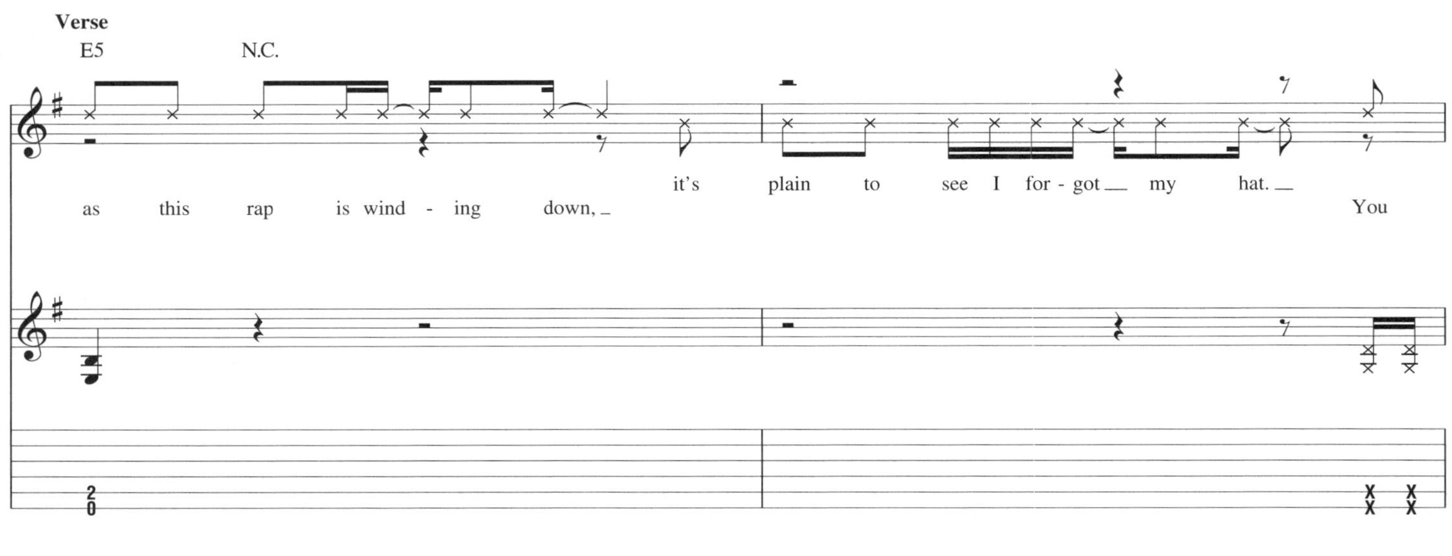
Verse
E5
N.C.
it's plain to see I for - got my hat.
as this rap is wind - ing down,
You

E5
F5
E♭5
F5
E5
N.C.
but we don't care, we just wan - na have...
know An - thrax is num - ber one,
P.M.

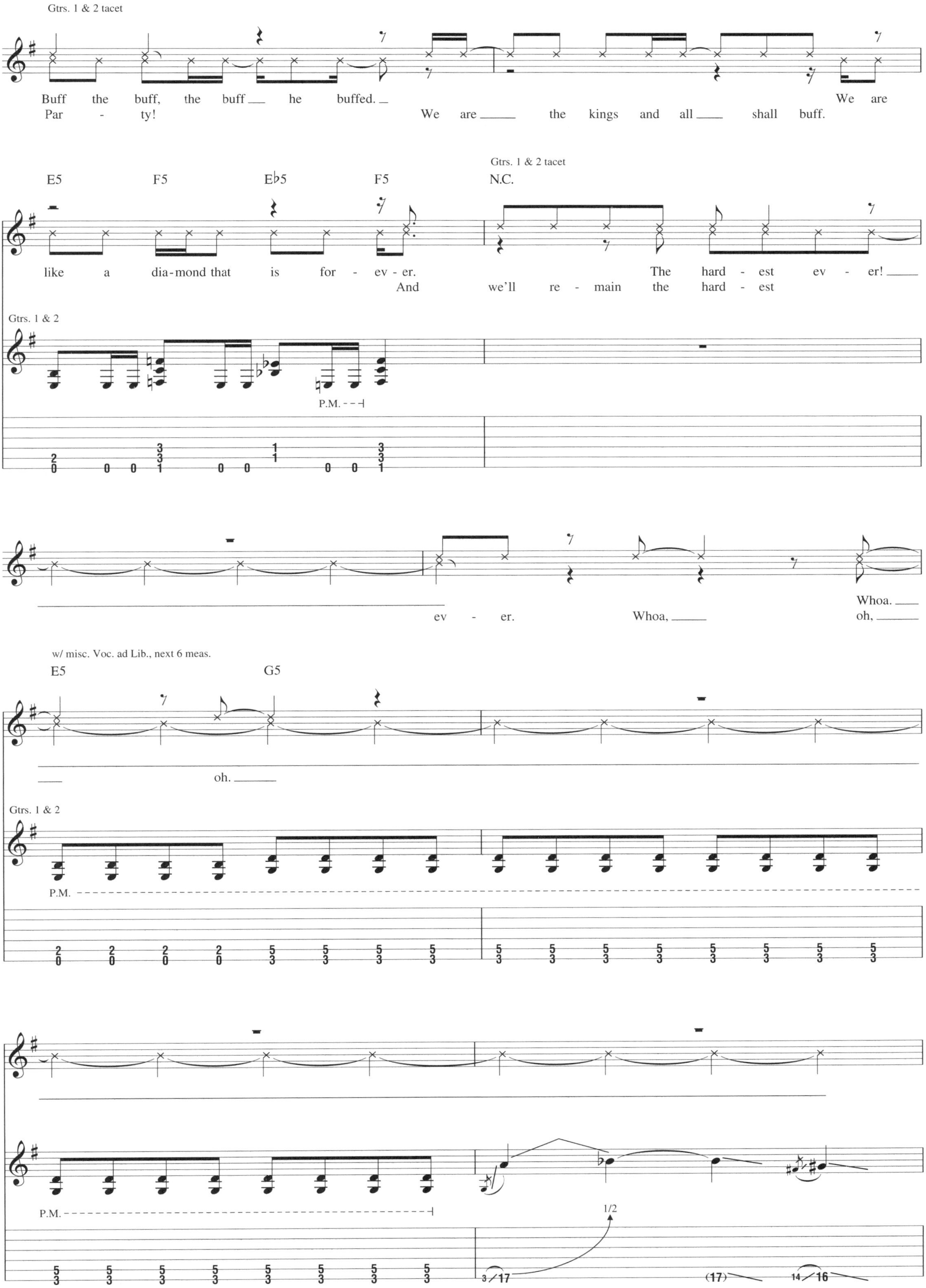

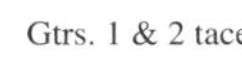

Gtrs. 1 & 2 tacet

Buff the buff, the buff he buffed. We are
Par - ty! We are the kings and all shall buff.

E5 F5 E♭5 F5

Gtrs. 1 & 2 tacet

N.C.

like a dia-mond that is for - ev - er. The hard - est ev - er!
And we'll re - main the hard - est

Gtrs. 1 & 2

P.M.

ev - er. Whoa, Whoa.
oh,

w/ misc. Voc. ad Lib., next 6 meas.

E5 G5

oh.

Gtrs. 1 & 2

P.M.

P.M.

1/2

Gtr. 2
let ring
Gtr. 1
w/ bar
-1/2
Outro
Gtr. 2 tacet
Gtr. 1
Gtr. 1 tacet
Spoken: He's a fuckin' bum.
-1
-1 1/2
*Slide while holding bar depressed.
Spoken: I can hear your fuckin' radio, you stupid shit!
Yeah!
Fuck that shit!
Fuck that shit!
Fuck that shit!
Fuck that shit!
Fuck that shit.
Yeah!
Fuck that shit!
6
Spoken: He's a fuckin' bum.
He's a fuckin' bum.
Fuck that shit!
Fuck that shit!
Yeah!
7

from *Persistence of Time*

Keep It in the Family

Words and Music by Joseph Bellardini, Frank Bello, Charlie Benante, Scott Rosenfeld and Daniel Spitz

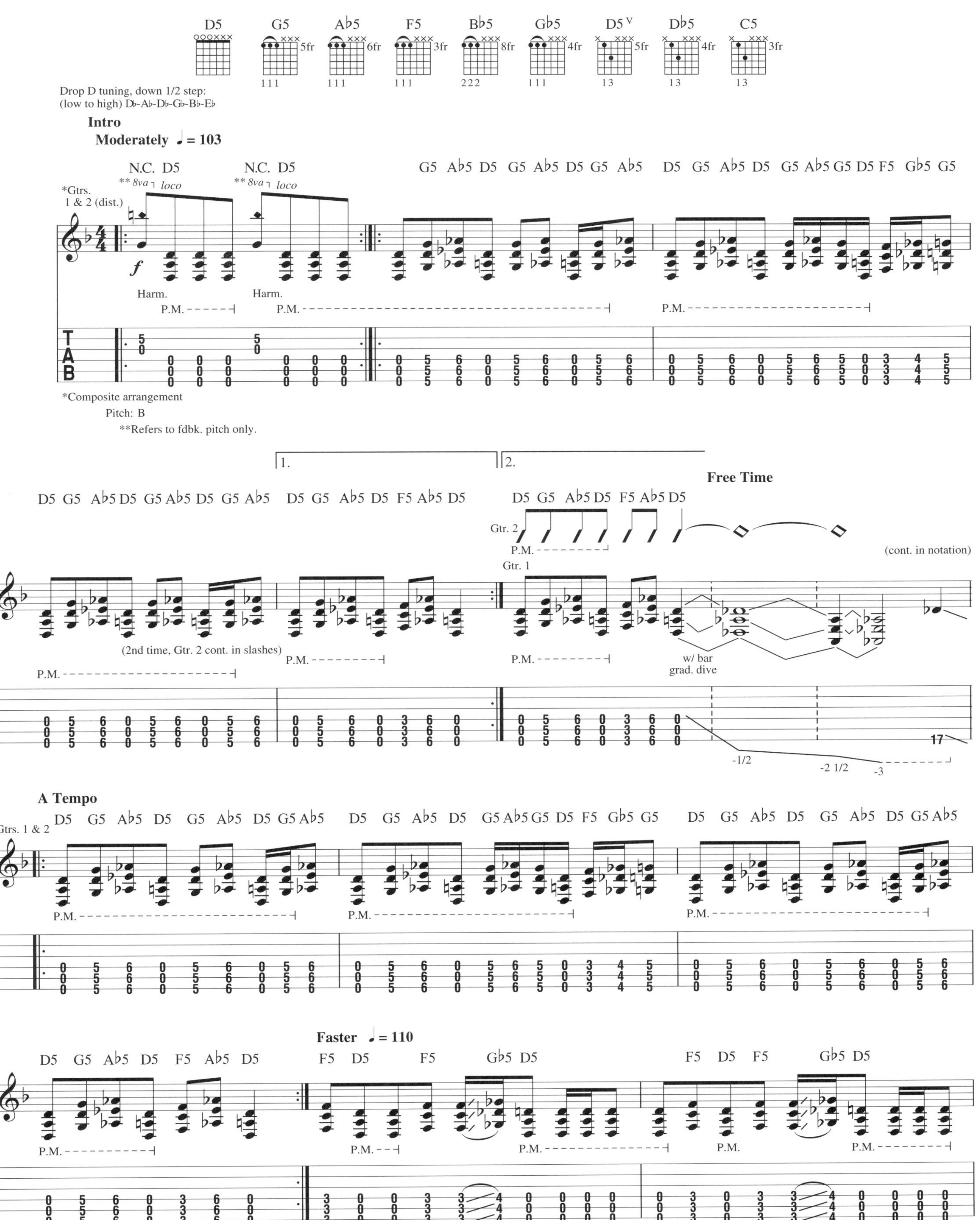

F5 D5 F5 Gb5 D5
F5 D5 F5 Gb5 D5
F5 D5 F5 Gb5 D5
Rhy. Fig. 1
P.M.
F5 D5 F5 Gb5 D5
F5 D5 F5 Gb5 D5
F5 D5 F5 Ab5 D5
Mm.
End Rhy. Fig. 1
* Verse
Gtrs. 1 & 2: w/ Rhy. Fig. 1 (3 1/2 times)
1. Mankind, the public enemy's not the man who speaks his mind.
The public enemy's the man that goes and acts blind,
searching for an answer that he'll never find.
An action from reaction and you can't make a retraction once you put your head out.
And then you're
3. Don't even try to tell me what you think is right, when to you blacks are niggers and Jews are kikes.
And you expect to be taken seriously, but your actions, they're more than curiously juvenile.
You emulate what you hate, and you don't even know why you feel this way. 'Cause
*2nd time, slower ♩ = 116

Faster ♩ = 145
F5 D5 F5 G♭5 D5 F5 D5 N.C. E♭5 D5
think with your dick, but it can't shout.
own a - bil - i - ty to rea - son's like a tire gone flat.
2., 4. Yo, I
Gtrs. 1 & 2
P.M.
Verse
Faster ♩ = 154
Gtrs. 1 & 2: w/ Rhy. Fig. 1 (2 times)
F5 D5 F5 G♭5 D5 F5 D5 F5 G♭5 D5 F5 D5 F5 G♭5 D5 F5 D5 F5 A♭5 D5
try to un-der-stand what the hell is go-in' on. I can't im-a-gine how things ev-er got so far gone. You
F5 D5 F5 G♭5D5 F5 D5 F5 G♭5 D5 F5 D5 F5 G♭5 D5 F5 D5 F5 A♭5 D5
sep-'ra-tists, say you want your own state. I'll give them a state, a state of un-con-scious-ness.
Faster ♩ = 160
D5 D♭5 C5 B5 D5 D♭5 C5 B5 D5 D♭5 C5 B5 D5 N.C.
Ret - ri-bu - tion, no so-lu - tion, con - sti-tu - tion. Dis-
Gtrs. 1 & 2
P.M.
D5 D♭5 C5 B5 D5 D♭5 C5 B5 D5 D♭5 C5 B5 D5 N.C.
cri - mi-na - tion, through the na - tion, rain - ing hat - red.
P.M.

Pre-Chorus
Faster ♩ = 170
Eb5 D5 Eb5 D5 Eb5 D5
(I yell...) When there's schis - m you must rebel. (I yell...) So
P.M.
Db5 C5 Eb5 D5 Eb5 D5
you'll hear. (I yell...) I re - fuse to live in your hell.
P.M.
Faster ♩ = 175
Eb5 D5 Db5 C5 D5 Ab5 G5 D5
(I am...) What you fear. I'm the truth,
P.M.
Chorus
Db5 C5 D5 Ab5 G5 D5
I don't keep it in the fa - mi - ly. Live your life, take some one else.
Rhy. Fig. 2
End Rhy. Fig. 2
P.M.

Gtrs. 1 & 2: w/ Rhy. Fig. 2 (1 3/4 times)
D♭5 C5 D5 A♭5 G5 D5
Keep it in the fa - mi - ly.
The real world's out - side your door.
D♭5 C5
You can't keep it in the fa - mi - ly.
You've got the long - est way
1.
D5 A♭5 G5 D5 E♭5 D5 E♭5 D5 E♭5
to fall.
Keep it in the, keep it in the, keep it in the
Gtrs. 1 & 2
P.M.
D5 E♭5 D5 F5 E♭5
fa - mi - ly.
rit.
2.
D5 A♭5 G5 D5
to fall.
Faster ♩ = 185
B♭5 F5 D5
When you keep it in the, when
B♭5 F5 D5 B♭5 F5 D5
you keep it in the, when you keep it in the
1.
B♭5 F5 D5
fa - mi - ly.
When
2.
F5 G♭5 G5 D5
- mi - ly.
Yeah.
Gtr. 3 (dist.)
w/ delay
Gtrs. 1 & 2
P.M.
(cont. in slashes)

Guitar Solo
D5 B♭5 F5 D5
Gtrs. 1 & 2
P.M.
Gtr. 3
*w/ octaver
*Set for one octave below.
H
steady gliss.
octaver off
8va
w/ octaver
D5 B♭5 F5 G♭5 G5 D♭5 C5

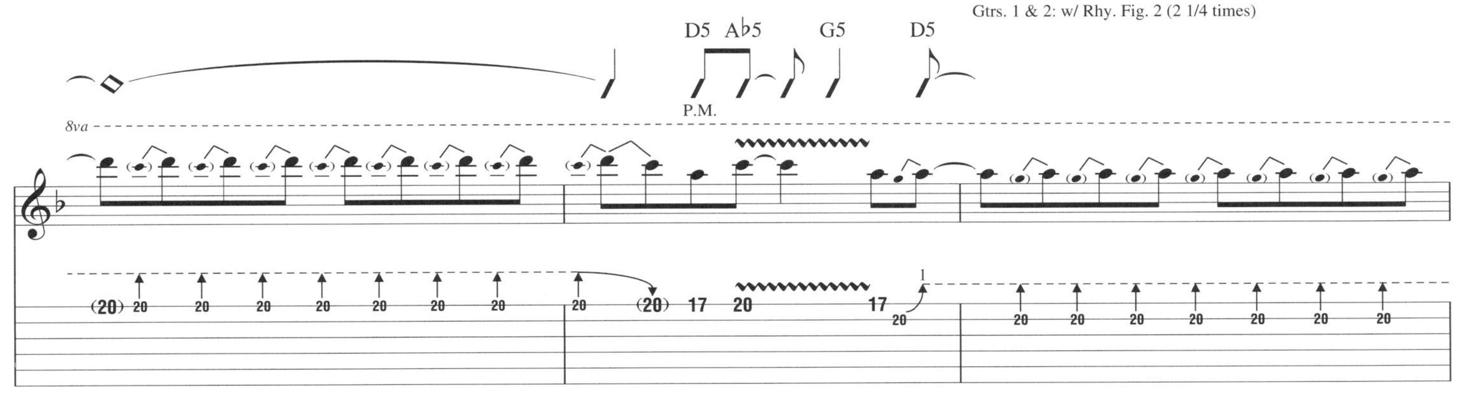
Gtrs. 1 & 2: w/ Rhy. Fig. 2 (2 1/4 times)
D5
A♭5
G5
D5
P.M.
8va

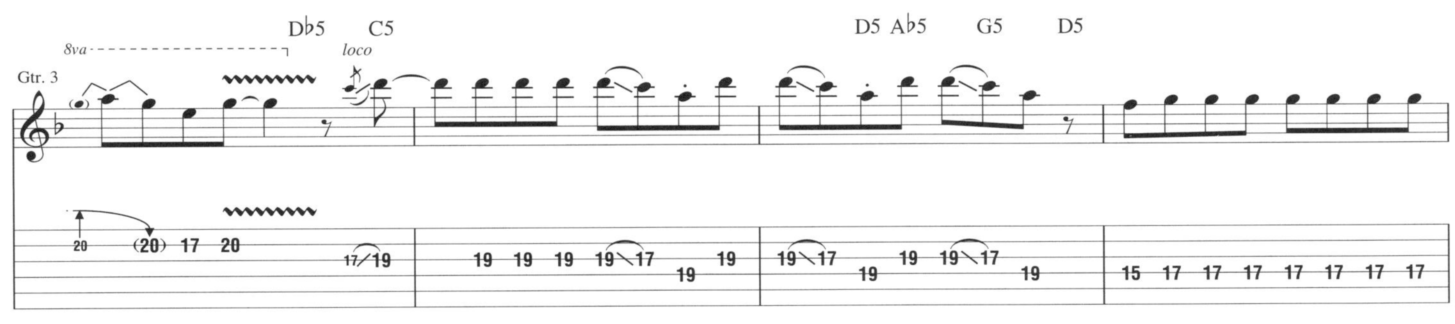
D♭5
C5
D5
A♭5
G5
D5
8va
loco
Gtr. 3

D♭5
C5
D5
A♭5
G5
D5
octaver off
steady gliss.
P.M.

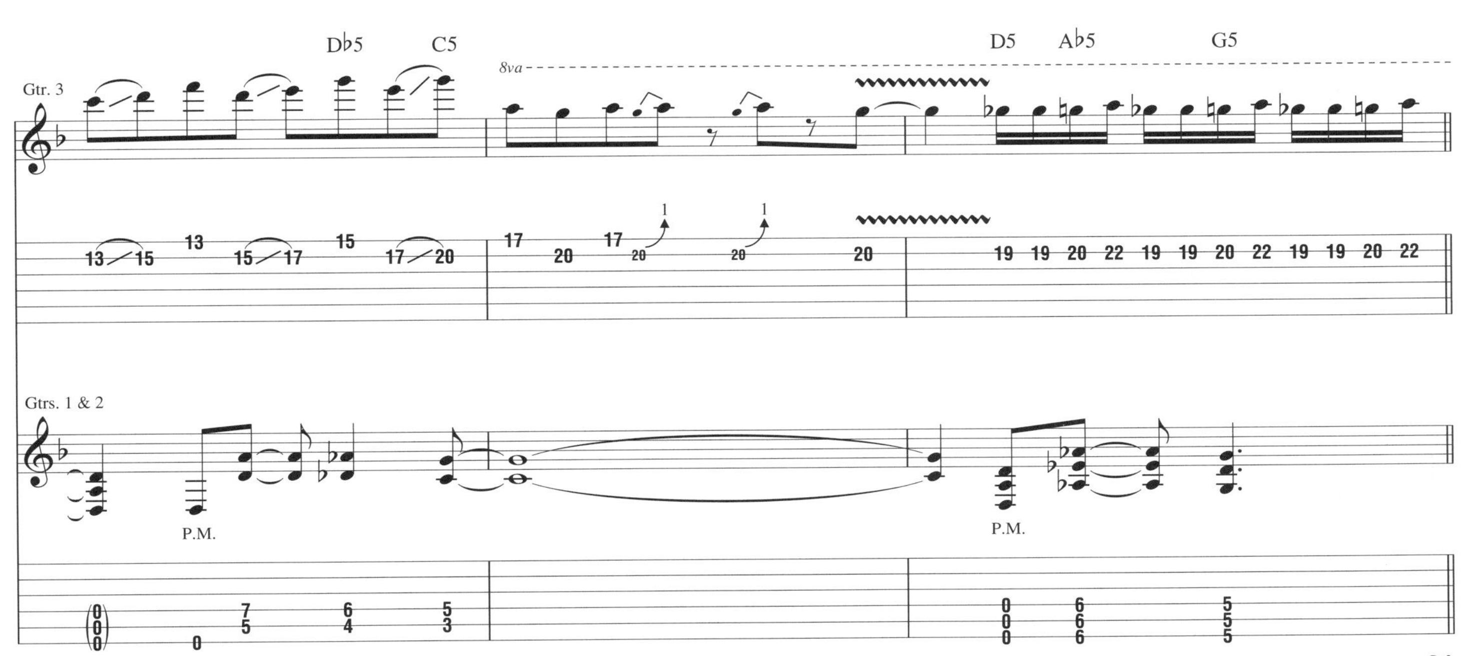
D♭5
C5
D5
A♭5
G5
Gtr. 3
8va
Gtrs. 1 & 2
P.M.
P.M.

Interlude
Slower ♩ = 103
D5 F5 D5
F5 A♭5 D5
F5 A♭5 D5
F5 A♭5 D5
8va
Gtr. 3
Gtrs. 1 & 2
Rhy. Fig. 3
End Rhy. Fig. 3
P.M.
Bridge
Gtrs. 1 & 2: w/ Rhy. Fig. 3 (3 times)
Gtr. 3 tacet
F5 A♭5 D5
Act - ing out of pure cold hat - red 'cause of what an - oth - er's race is, col - or of an - oth - er's face is
diff - 'rent, and your own fru - stra - tions. Tak - ing on a vi - 'lent na - ture full of hate, so full of hate. You'd
kill a man is that your fate. Your street be - comes a po - lice state. Why the hell do you hate?
G5 A♭5 D5
Spoken: One, two, three, four, five, six,
(Hate! Hate! Hate! Hate! Hate! Hate!
Gtrs. 1 & 2
P.M.

D5 G5 Ab5 D5 G5 Ab5 D5 G5 Ab5 D5 G5 Ab5 N.C.
I'm not gon - na stand for it. Some - one's gon - na pay for it.
seven, eight, nine, ten.)
Hate! Hate! Hate! Hate!)
P.M.
Free Time
Faster ♩ = 185
Eb5 D5 Db5 C5 D5 Ab5 G5 D5
I yell, we reb - el. We're the truth,
P.M.
Chorus
Gtrs. 1 & 2: w/ Rhy. Fig. 2 (3 times)
Db5 C5 Ab5 G5 D5
you'll nev - er keep it in the fa - mi - ly. Live your life, take some one else.
Db5 C5 Ab5 G5 D5
Keep it in the fa - mi - ly. The real world's out - side your door.
Db5 C5 Ab5 G5 D5
You can't keep it in the fa - mi - ly. You've got the long - est way to fall.

Db5 C5 Ab5 G5 D5
Keep it in the fa - mi - ly. I'm the thing that you most fear.
Gtrs. 1 & 2
P.M.
I don't keep it in the fa - mi - ly. I'm the truth that you won't hear.
Keep it in the fa - mi - ly. The real world's out - side your door.
You can't keep it in the fa - mi - ly. You got the long-est way to fall.

Faster ♩ = 200
B♭5 F5 D5
Keep it in the fa - mi - ly.
Rhy. Fig. 4
End Rhy. Fig. 4
P.M.
Gtrs. 1 & 2: w/ Rhy. Fig. 4
F5 G♭5 G5 D5
Keep it in the fa - mi - ly.
Outro
Gtrs. 1 & 2: w/ Rhy. Fig. 4 (1 3/4 times)
1.
2.
Gtrs. 1 & 2
E5
rit.
Free time
Begin fade
Fade out
*8va
Gtr. 1
w/ bar
+1/2
-1/2
Pitch: A
*Refers to fdbk. pitch only.
Gtr. 2
-2 1/2

from *Spreading the Disease*

Madhouse

Words and Music by Joseph Bellardini, Frank Bello, Charlie Benante, Scott Rosenfeld and Daniel Spitz

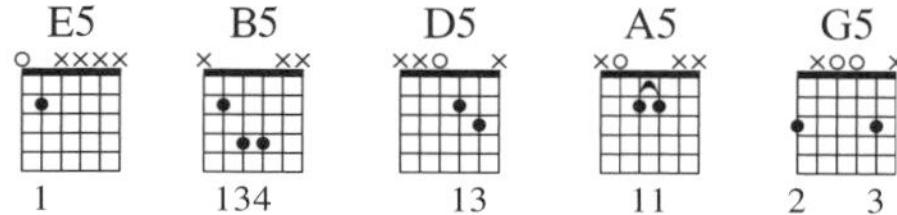

Spoken: It's time for your medication, Mister Brown. (Maniacal laughter:) Ooh, hoo, ha, ha, ha...

Intro

Moderately fast ♩ = 160

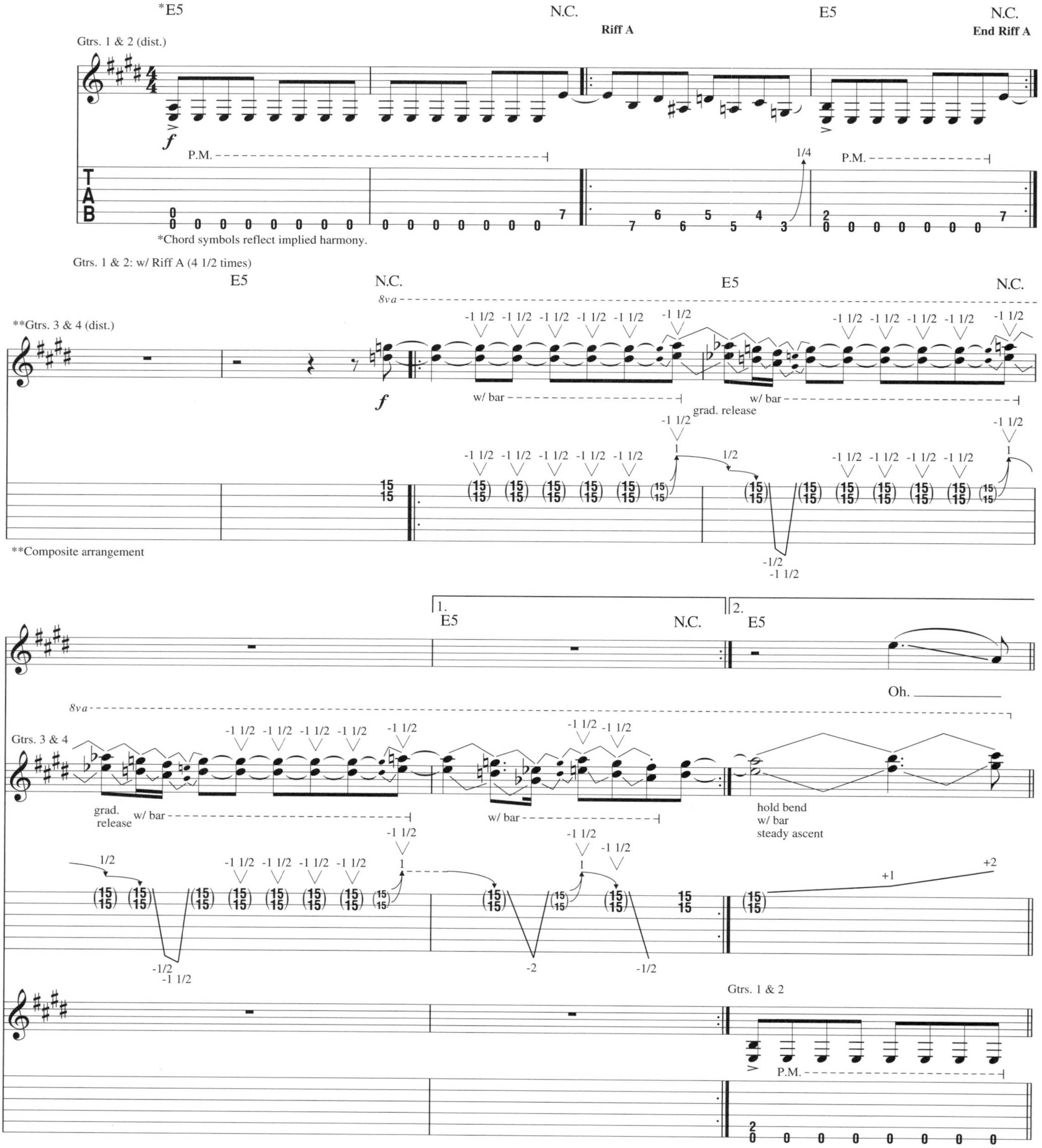

*E5 N.C. Riff A E5 N.C. End Riff A

Gtrs. 1 & 2 (dist.)

f

P.M.

1/4

P.M.

*Chord symbols reflect implied harmony.

Gtrs. 1 & 2: w/ Riff A (4 1/2 times)

E5 N.C. E5 N.C.

8va

**Gtrs. 3 & 4 (dist.)

f

w/ bar

grad. release

w/ bar

**Composite arrangement

1. E5 N.C. 2. E5

Oh.

8va

Gtrs. 3 & 4

grad. release w/ bar

w/ bar

hold bend w/ bar steady ascent

Gtrs. 1 & 2

P.M.

Verse
Gtrs. 3 & 4 tacet
B5 D5 A5 B5 G5 D5/A
1. White coats to bind me, out of con - trol,
2. My fears be - hind me, what can I do?
Gtrs. 1 & 2
P.M.
B5 D5/A A5 B5 G5 D5/A
I live a - lone in - side my mind.
My dreams haunt my sleep at night. Oh, no.
Rhy. Fig. 1
End Rhy. Fig. 1
P.M.
Gtr. 1: w/ Rhy. Fig. 1
B5 D5/A A5 B5 G5 D5/A
World of con - fu - sion, air filled with noise,
Won't learn their les - son, white fills my eyes,
Gtr. 2
Rhy. Fig. 2
End Rhy. Fig. 2
P.M.
Gtr. 2: w/ Rhy. Fig. 2
B5 D5/A A5 B5 G5 D5/A
who says that my life's such a crime?
and on - ly then they see the light.
Gtr. 1
P.M.

3rd time, Gtr. 3: w/ Fill 1
3rd time, Gtr. 4 tacet
E5 F E5 F E5 F E5 F(♭5)
Trapped in this night - mare, I wish I'd wake,
Gtrs. 1 & 2
Riff B
P.M.
E5 F E5 F E5 F E5 C5 G♯5
1., 3. as
2. and
my whole life be-gins to shake.
End Riff B
Gtrs. 1 & 2: w/ Riff B
E5 F E5 F E5 F E5 F(♭5)
Four walls sur - round me, an emp - ty gaze,
E5 F E5 F E5 F E5 C5 G♯5
I can't find my way out of this maze. And I don't
Pre-Chorus
A5 B♭5/A A5 B♭5/A A5 C5 B5 B♭5
care, fall in, fall out. Gone with-out a doubt. I
(Help me.)
Gtrs. 1 & 2
Rhy. Fig. 3
End Rhy. Fig. 3
*Gang vocals
Fill 1
Gtr. 3
8va
P.H.
w/ bar
grad. dive
Pitch: E
-3 1/2

Gtr. 1: w/ Rhy. Fig. 3
A5
B♭5/A
A5
B♭5/A
A5
C5 B5 B♭5
can't take the blame.
1., 3. They
2. I
don't feel the shame.
2. 'Cause
Gtr. 2
P.M.
Chorus
N.C.
E5
N.C.
E5
N.C.
1., 3. It's
(2.) it's
a mad - house
or so they claim.
It's
Gtrs. 1 & 2
1/4
P.M.
*Gang vocals
To Coda
1.
1st & 3rd times, Gtrs. 1 & 2: w/ Riff A (2 times)
2nd time, Gtrs. 1 & 2: w/ Riff A (1 1/2 times)
E5
N.C.
E5
a mad - house, oh, am I in - sane?
2.
E5
N.C.
E5
Gtrs. 1 & 2
I'm in - sane.
Gtr. 3
P.H.
w/ bar
grad. ascent
Pitch: F♯
-2 1/2
-3 1/2
-2 1/2
-1
Guitar Solo
B5
D5
A5
B5
G5
D5
Rhy. Fig. 4
End Rhy. Fig. 4
grad. bend
1 hold bend
P.M.

Gtrs. 1 & 2: w/ Rhy. Fig. 4 (3 times)
B5
D5
A5
B5
G5
D5
P.M.
P.H.
P.M.
P.H.
P.H.
w/ bar
w/ bar
P.H.
w/ bar
grad. dive
Pitch: G♯
F♯
F♯
Gtr. 3
Gtr. 4
divisi
Pitch: F♯
D.S. al Coda
8va
loco
grad. bend
P.M.
P.M.
grad.bend
Coda
E5
N.C.
I'm in - sane.
Mad,
mad - house.
Mad, mad, mad, mad - house.
(Mad! Mad! Mad!)
Gtrs. 1 & 2

from *Sound of White Noise*

Only

Words and Music by Frank Bello, Charlie Benante, John Bush, Scott Rosenfeld, Daniel Spitz

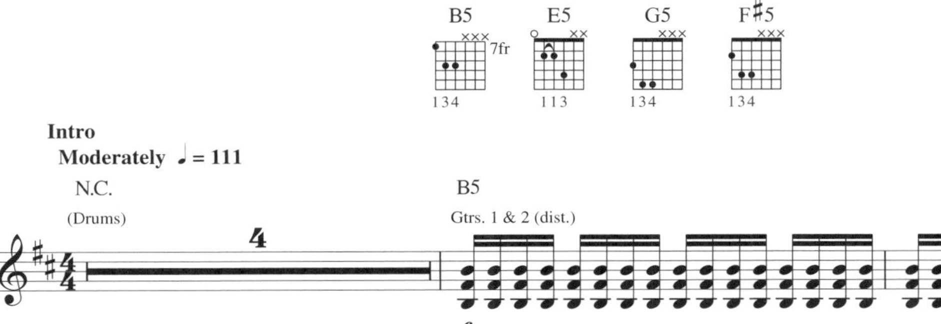

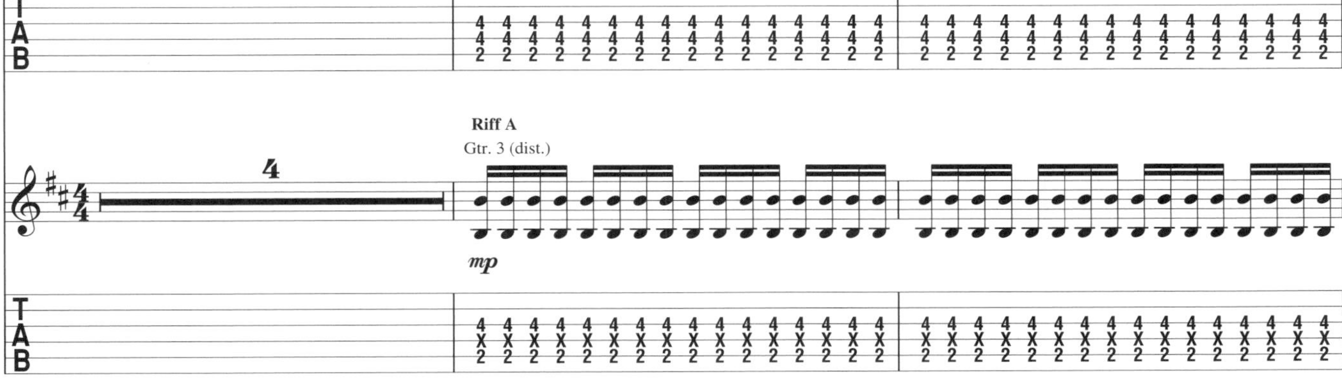

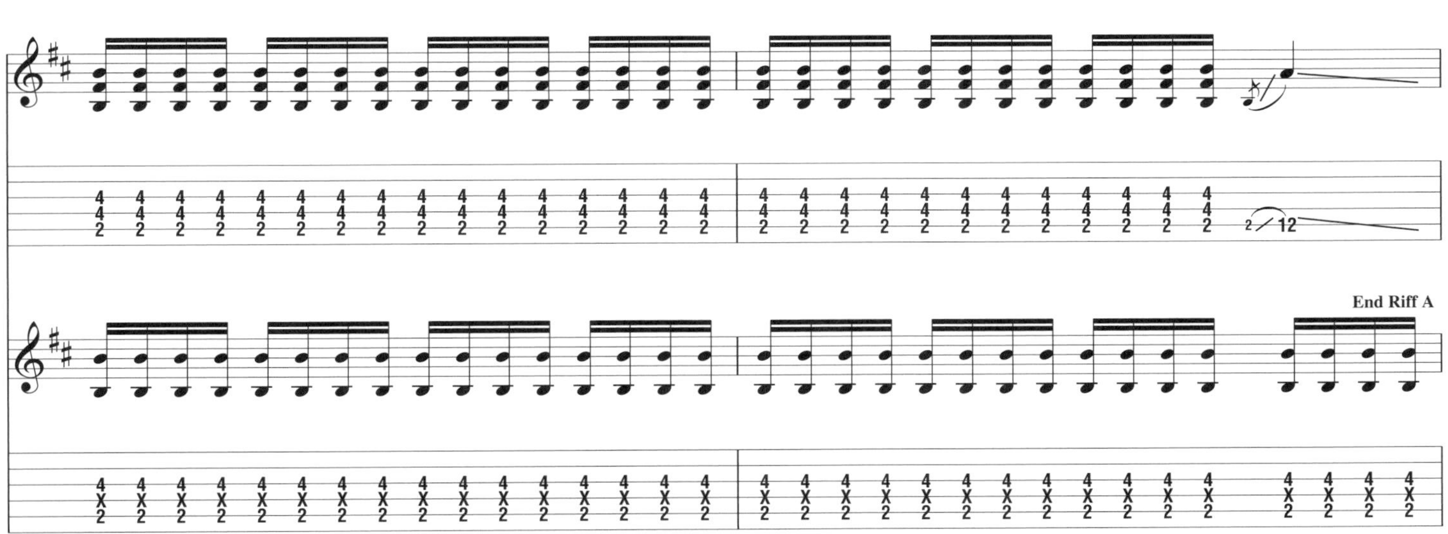

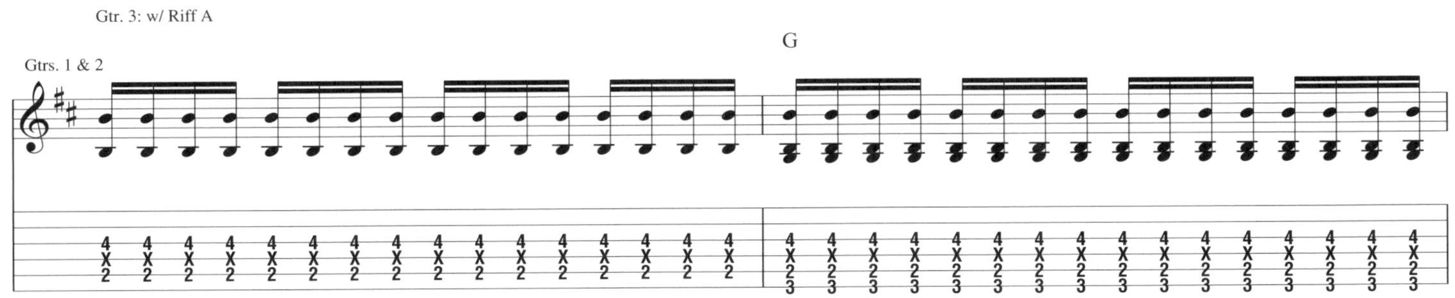

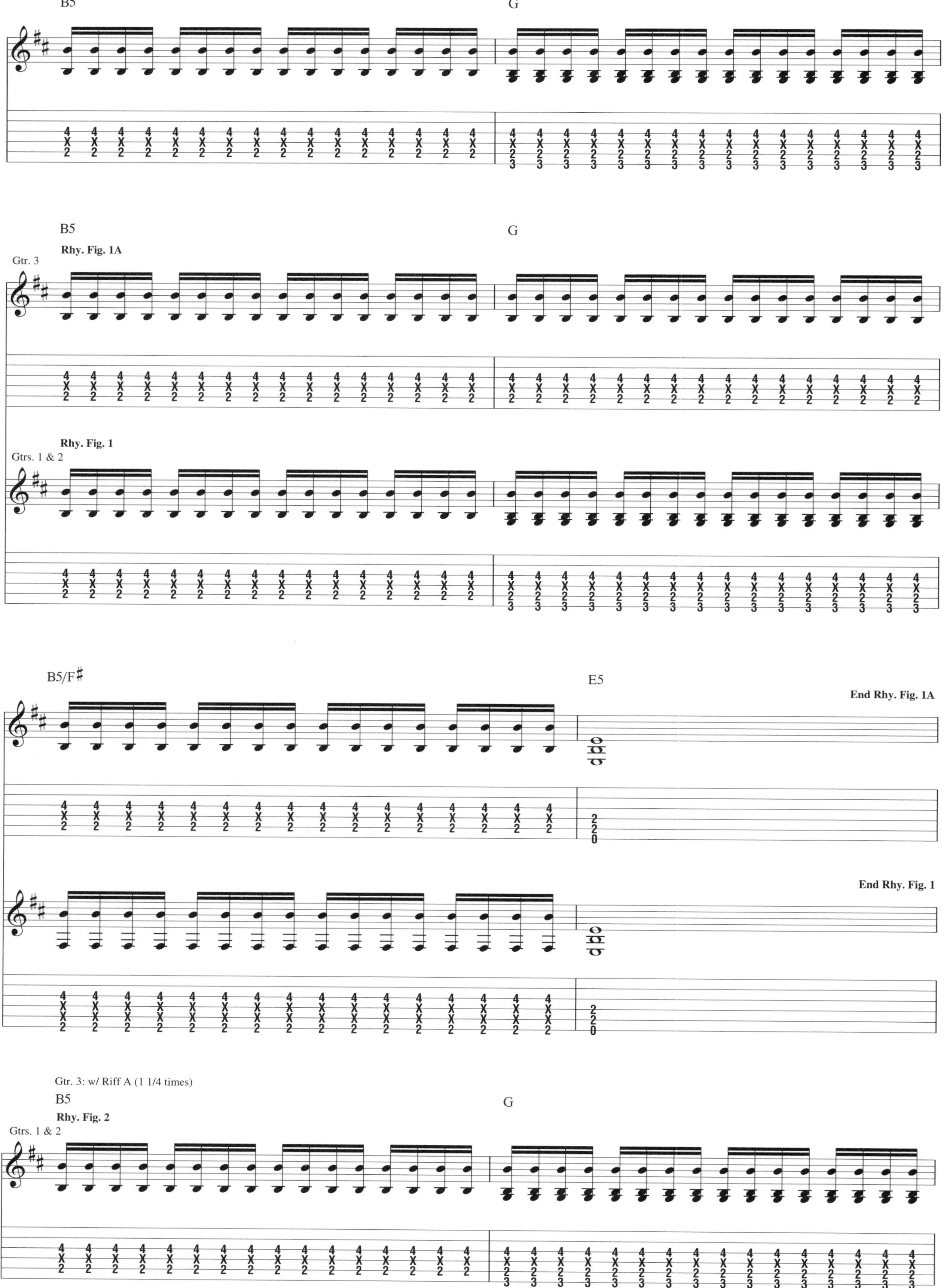
B5
G
B5
G
Rhy. Fig. 1A
Gtr. 3
Rhy. Fig. 1
Gtrs. 1 & 2
B5/F♯
E5
End Rhy. Fig. 1A
End Rhy. Fig. 1
Gtr. 3: w/ Riff A (1 1/4 times)
B5
G
Rhy. Fig. 2
Gtrs. 1 & 2

B5/F♯
E5
End Rhy. Fig. 2
P.M.

Verse
*B5
D5
B5
D5
B5
D5
B5
D5
1. Ev - 'ry - thing is per - fect.
2. Clas - sic ways to live here,
Rhy. Fig. 3
P.M.
*Chord symbols reflect implied harmony.

2nd time, Gtr. 4: w/ Fill 1
Bm
G♯5
G5
Ev - 'ry - thing is sick, and that's it.
com - pro - mise for me, yeah.
End Rhy. Fig. 3
P.M.
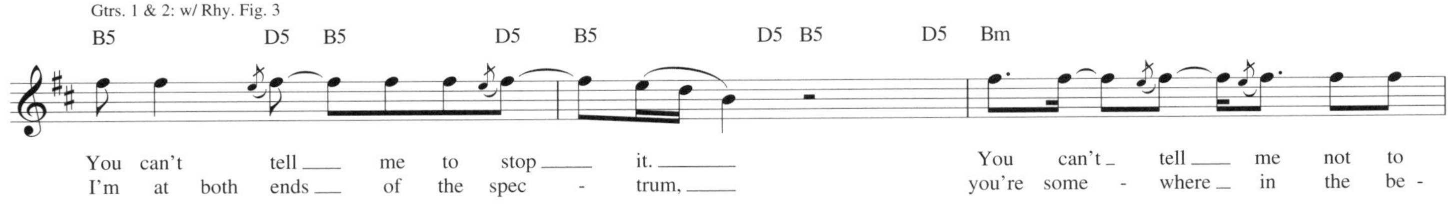
Gtrs. 1 & 2: w/ Rhy. Fig. 3
B5
D5
B5
D5
B5
D5
B5
D5
Bm
You can't tell me to stop it. You can't tell me not to
I'm at both ends of the spec - trum, you're some - where in the be -

Fill 1
Gtr. 4 (dist.)
f
P.S.

G♯5
G5
quit, and that's it.
tween. Ah, come clean.
Re -
Pre-Chorus
Bm7
G♯(♭5)
volve a - round your - self. It's you and no one else. Hard for me to stay.
Gtrs. 1 & 2
G5
Bm7
Swing - ing moods that change from calm - ness to de - ranged.
let ring
let ring
G♯(♭5)
G5
2nd time, Gtrs. 1 & 2: w/ Rhy. Fill 1
E5
Un - pre - dict - a - ble, un - pre-dict - a - ble. You would see if
let ring
let ring
Rhy. Fill 1
Gtrs. 1 & 2

Chorus
Gtrs. 1 & 2: w/ Rhy. Fig. 1
Gtr. 3: w/ Rhy. Fig. 1A
B5
G
B5/F♯
on - ly you had - n't tak - en things out of my
E5
Gtrs. 1 & 2: w/ Rhy. Fig. 2
Gtr. 3: w/ Riff A (1 1/4 times)
B5
G
hands. On - ly you nev - er
1.
B5/F♯
E5
want - ed to un - der - stand.
2.
E5
stand.
Gtrs. 1 & 2
Interlude
B5
(cont. in slashes)

Guitar Solo

B5
Gtrs. 1 & 2
Gtr. 4
w/ wah-wah
P.H.
P.H.
P.M.
1/2
1
1/2
1/2
Pitch: D♯
A

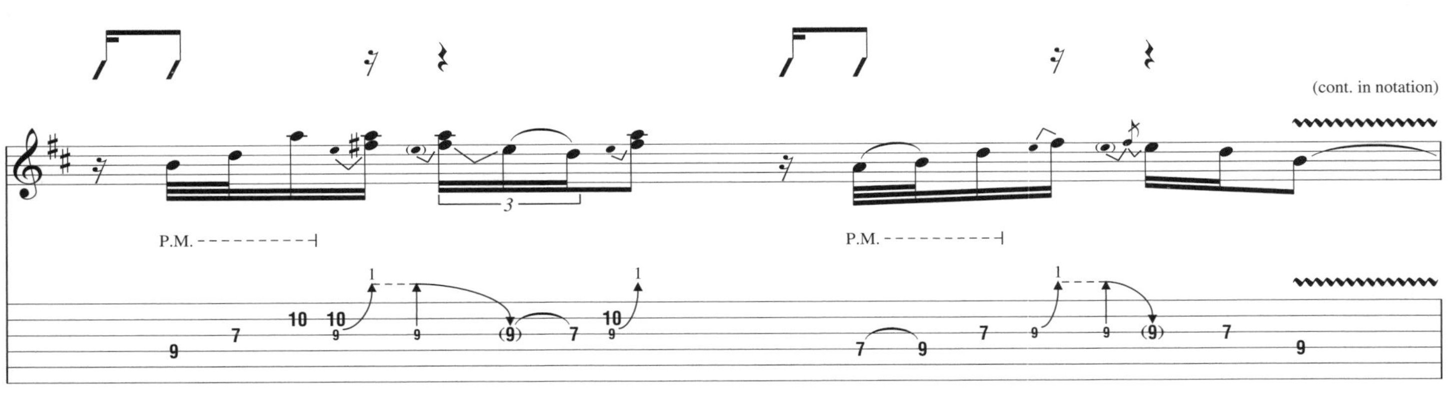
(cont. in notation)
P.M.
P.M.
1
1
1

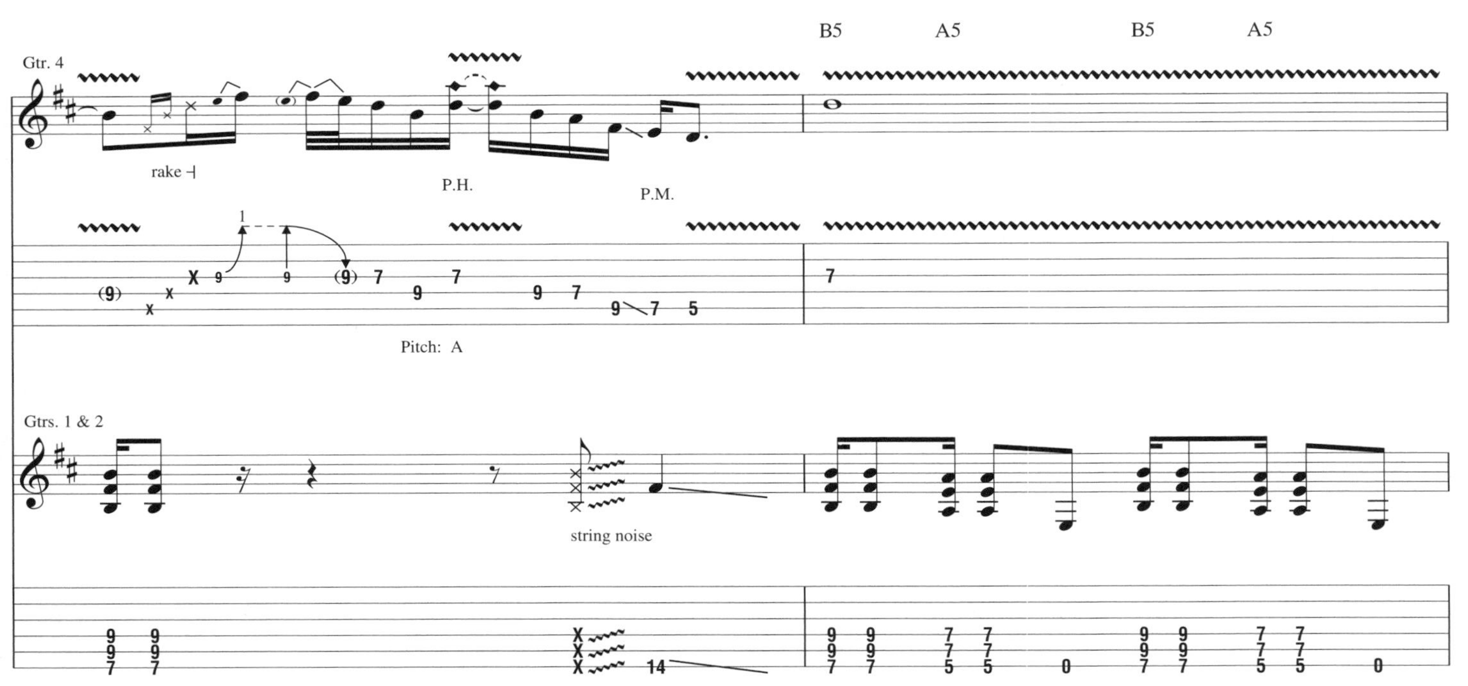
B5
A5
B5
A5
Gtr. 4
rake
P.H.
P.M.
1
Pitch: A
Gtrs. 1 & 2
string noise

B5
A5
B5
A5
B5
A5
B5
A5
B5
A5
B5
A5
B5
hold bend
hold bend
P.H.
Pitch: F♯
D♯
hold bend

Bm
B5
P.M.
G5
F♯5
let ring
(cont. in slashes)
E5
B5
G5
Gtrs. 1 & 2
Gtr. 4
grad. bend
1 1/2
F♯5
E5
8va

Chorus
Gtrs. 1 & 2: w/ Rhy. Fig. 1 (2 times)
Gtr. 3: w/ Rhy. Fig. 1A (2 times)
Gtr. 4 tacet
B5
G
B5/F♯
E5
On - ly you had - n't tak - en things out of my hands.
8va
loco
P.S.
B5
G
B5/F♯
E5
On - ly you nev - er want - ed to un - der - stand.
B5
G5
F♯5
On - ly you had - n't tak - en things out of my
Rhy. Fig. 4
Gtrs. 1 & 2
E5
B5
G5
hands. On - ly you nev - er
(Out of my hands.)

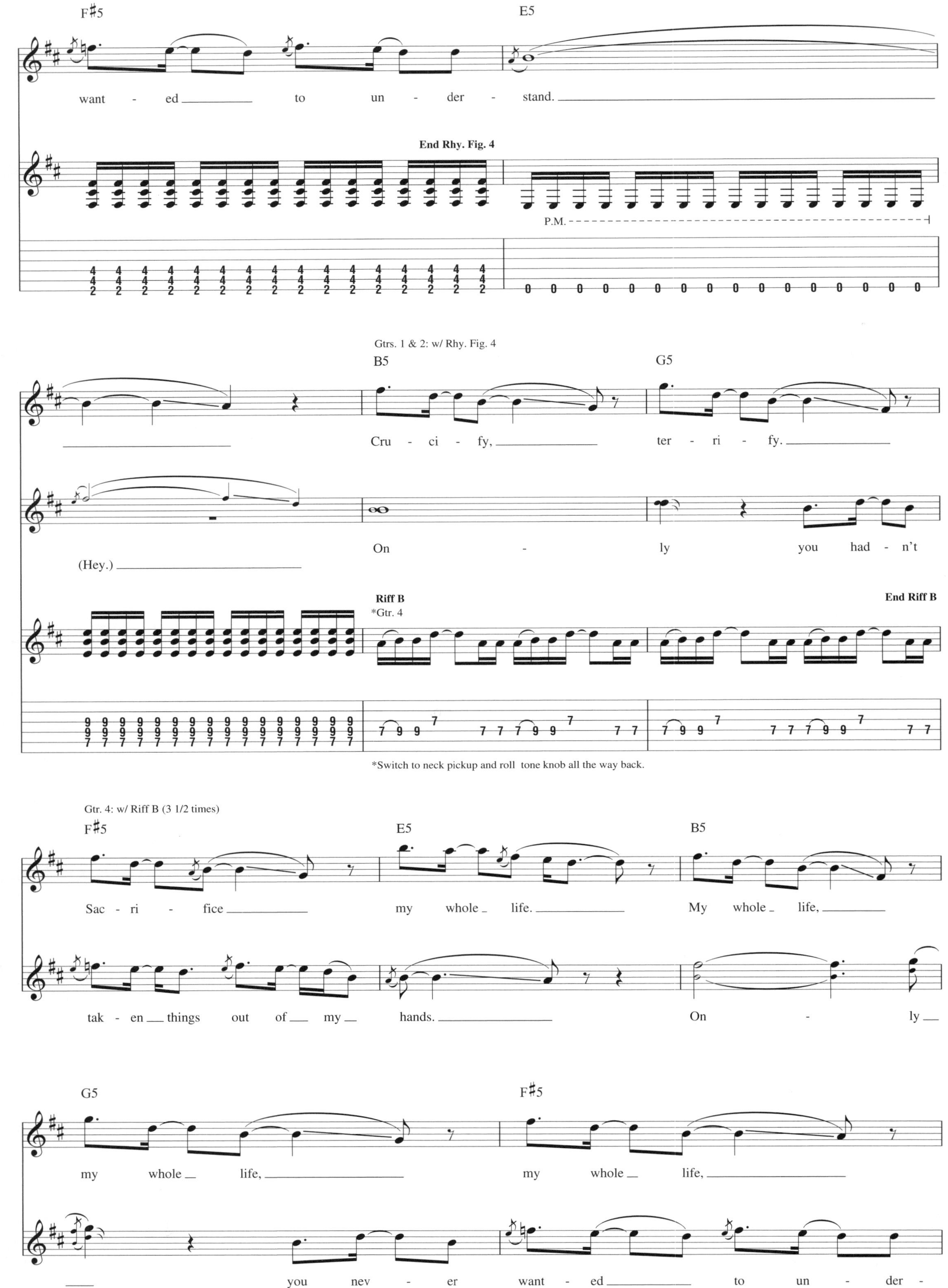
F#5
E5
want - ed to un - der - stand.
End Rhy. Fig. 4
P.M.
Gtrs. 1 & 2: w/ Rhy. Fig. 4
B5
G5
Cru - ci - fy, ter - ri - fy.
(Hey.)
On - ly you had - n't
Riff B
*Gtr. 4
End Riff B
*Switch to neck pickup and roll tone knob all the way back.
Gtr. 4: w/ Riff B (3 1/2 times)
F#5
E5
B5
Sac - ri - fice my whole life. My whole life,
tak - en things out of my hands. On - ly
G5
F#5
my whole life, my whole life,
you nev - er want - ed to un - der -

E5

my whole life.

stand.

Gtrs. 1 & 2

Outro

B5 A5 E5 B5 A5 E5 B5 A5 E5 B5 A5 E5

On - ly. If on - ly. If

Rhy. Fig. 5

End Rhy. Fig. 5

Gtrs. 1 & 2: w/ Rhy. Fig. 5 (2 times)

B5 A5 E5 B5 A5 E5 B5 A5 E5 B5 A5 E5 B5 A5 E5 B5 A5 E5 B5 A5 E5 B5 A5 E5

on - ly. If on - ly. I can't con - tain my - self. I can't con - tain my - self. I just can't

B5 A5 E5 B5 A5 E5 B5

take my - self.

Gtrs. 1 & 2

from *Among the Living*

A Skeleton in the Closet

Words and Music by Joseph Bellardini, Frank Bello, Charlie Benante, Scott Rosenfeld and Daniel Spitz

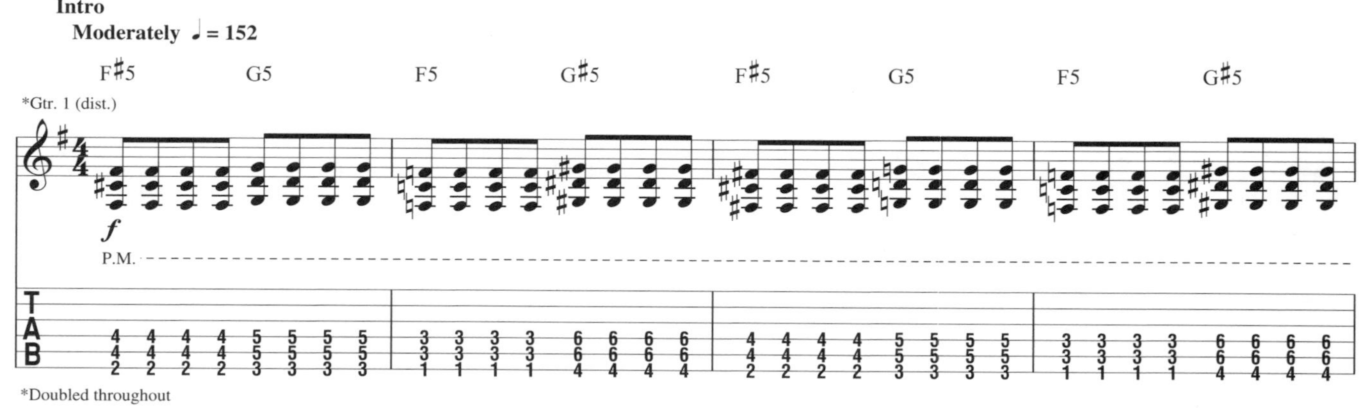

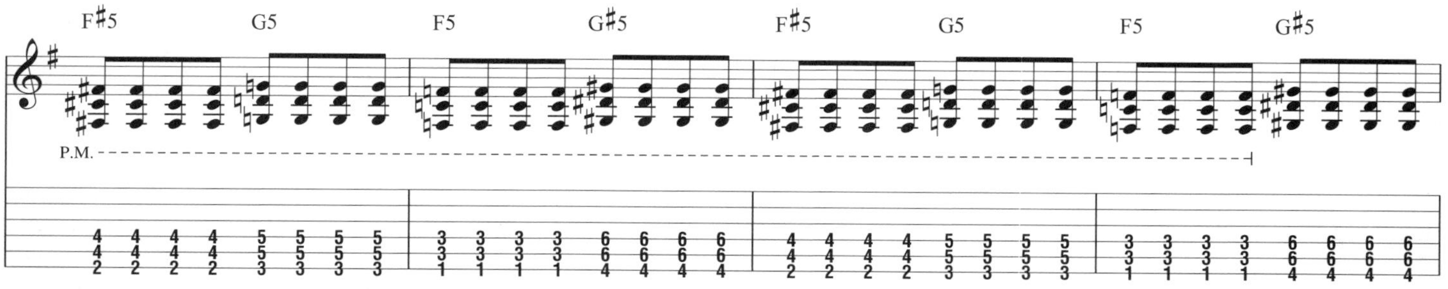

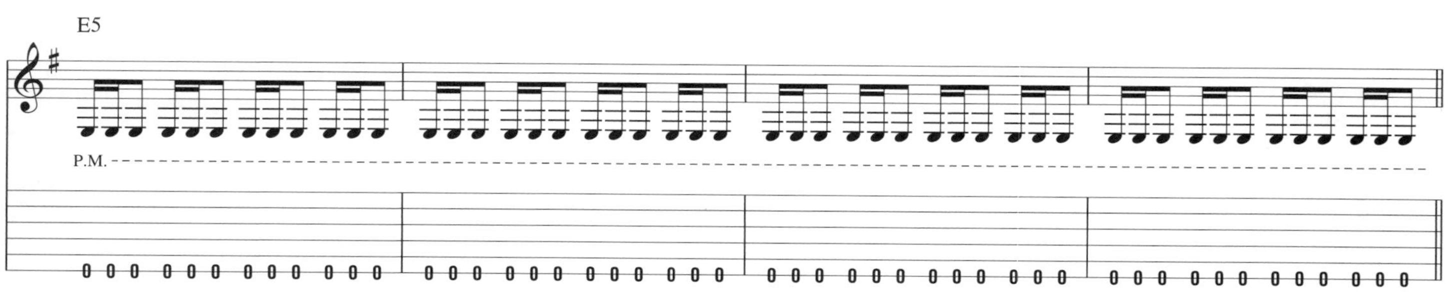

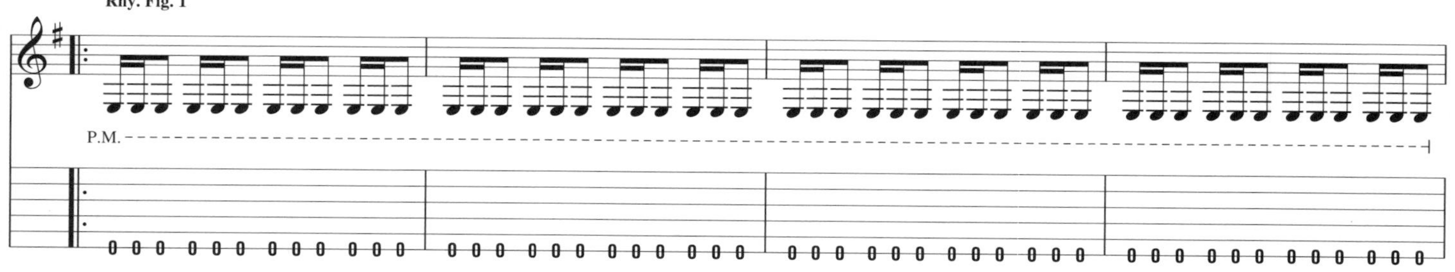

G5 F#5 E5 F#5 G5 F#5 A5 C5 G5 F#5 E5 F#5 G5 F#5 A5 C5
End Rhy. Fig. 1
P.M.
Verse
E5
1. All A - mer - i - can, e - vil game of ex - tor - tion.
Rhy. Fig. 2
P.M.
G5 F#5 E5 F#5 G5 F#5 A5 C5 G5 F#5 E5 F#5 G5 F#5 A5 C5
End Rhy. Fig. 2
Gtr. 1: w/ Rhy. Fig. 2 (3 times)
E5
Sick old man, and who would guess he was once S. S.?
G5 F#5 E5 F#5 G5 F#5 A5 C5 G5 F#5 E5 F#5 G5 F#5 A5 C5
A
E5
dead - ly fas - ci - na - tion of a mad - man's so - lu - tion.

G5 F#5 E5 F#5 G5 F#5 A5 C5 G5 F#5 E5 F#5 G5 F#5 A5 C5
E5
Six mil - lion dead, poi - son tales pol - lute his head.
G5 F#5 E5 F#5 G5 F#5 A5 C5 G5 F#5 E5 F#5 G5 F#5 A5 C5
Pre-Chorus
2nd time, Gtr. 2: w/ Fill 1
3rd time, Gtr. 3: w/ Fill 2
E5 F#5 B5 A#5 E5 F#5 E5 F#5 E5 F#5 B5 A#5 E5 F#5 E5 F#5
Tell me a sto - ry. A real good sto - ry.
(Will ya? Will ya? I won't leave 'til ya...)
Rhy. Fig. 3
Gtr. 1
End Rhy. Fig. 3
E5 F#5 B5 A#5 E5 F#5 E5 F#5 E5 F#5 B5 A#5 E5 F#5 E5 F#5
Spill your guts, old man. Leave out an - y se - crets.
(Hid - ing in the...
Fill 1
Gtr. 2
Fill 2
Gtr. 3
w/ bar
slack

Chorus
*E5
A5
E5
A♯5
An - y skel - e - tons,
all your oth - er sins,
an - y skel - e - tons.
(In the clos - et!)
Riff A
End Riff A
P.M.
*Chord symbols reflect implied harmony.
1st & 2nd times, Gtr. 1: w/ Riff A (2 3/4 times)
3rd time, Gtr. 1: w/ Riff A (5 times)
An - y skel - e - tons,
an - y mis - for - tunes,
an - y skel - e - tons.
(Hid - ing in the clos - et!)
To Coda 2
An - y skel - e - tons,
an - y skel - e - tons.
To Coda 1
Interlude
(In the clos - et!)
Gtr. 1
Gtr. 1: w/ Rhy. Fig. 1
G5
F♯5 E5 F♯5
F♯5 A5 C5

Verse
Gtr. 1: w/ Rhy. Fig. 2 (4 times)
E5
2. It's in - san - i - ty, pup - pet mas - ter, boy or Na - zi.
G5 F♯5 E5 F♯5 G5 F♯5 A5 C5 G5 F♯5 E5 F♯5 G5 F♯5 A5 C5
Gtr. 2 (dist.)
f
P.M.
Gtr. 2 tacet
E5
Apt pu - pil, he hears the screams. Night - mare turns in - to a dream.
G5 F♯5 E5 F♯5 G5 F♯5 A5 C5 G5 F♯5 E5 F♯5 G5 F♯5 A5 C5
8va
loco
Gtr. 3 (dist.)
*pp f
*Vol. swell
Gtr. 3 tacet
E5
Ha - tred lives, boil - ing in - side. Deal - ing death, it's bum - i - cide.

G5
F♯5 E5 F♯5
G5
F♯5 A5
C5
G5
F♯5 E5 F♯5
G5
F♯5 A5 C5
Gtr. 2
hold bend
E5
In too deep, the sa-cred stand but it won't keep.
let ring
hold bend
D.S. al Coda 1
G5
F♯5 E5 F♯5
G5
F♯5 A5
C5
G5
F♯5
E5
F♯5
G5
F♯5 A5 C5
Yow!
let ring
Coda 1
A♯5
N.C.
clos - et!)

Guitar Solo
B5 A#5 G5 E5 B5 A#5 G5 E5
Gtr. 2
8va
P.M.
Gtr. 1
Rhy. Fig. 4
End Rhy. Fig. 4
P.M.
Gtr. 1: w/ Rhy. Fig. 4
Gtr. 2 tacet
B5 A#5 G5 E5 B5 A#5 G5 E5
Gtrs. 3 & 4 (dist.)
f
P.M.
B5 E5 A#5 E5 G5 E5 B5 E5 A#5 E5 G5 E5
Gtrs. 3 & 4
8va
P.M. P.M. P.M. P.M. P.M. P.M. P.M.
Gtr. 1
Rhy. Fig. 5
End Rhy. Fig. 5
P.M. P.M. P.M. P.M. P.M. P.M. P.M. P.M.
Gtr. 1: w/ Rhy. Fig. 5
B5 E5 A#5 E5 G5 E5 B5 E5 A#5 E5
Gtrs. 3 & 4
8va
loco

G5 E5
Ah!
8va
Gtrs. 3 & 4
Gtr. 1
P.M.
Interlude
Gtrs. 3 & 4 tacet
F♯5 G5 F5 G♯5 E5
pp
Play 3 times

F♯5 G5 F5 G♯5 F♯5 G5 F5 G♯5 F♯5 G5 F5 G♯5 F♯5 G5 F5 G♯5

P.M.

F♯5 G5 F5 G♯5 F♯5 G5 F5 G♯5 F♯5 G5 F5 G♯5 F♯5 G5 F5 G♯5 E5

P.M.

Gtr. 1: w/ Rhy. Fig. 1

G5 F♯5 E5 F♯5 G5 F♯5 A5 C5 G5 F♯5 E5 F♯5 G5 F♯5 A5 C5

Verse

Gtr. 1: w/ Rhy. Fig. 2 (4 times)

E5

3. Truth comes out. Con - spir - a - cy, there's no doubt.

G5 F♯5 E5 F♯5 G5 F♯5 A5 C5

Gtr. 2

P.M. P.M. P.M. P.M. P.M. P.M. P.M. P.M.

Gtr. 2 tacet
E5
life is ru - ined, but no, not yet. He's still got one card in the deck.

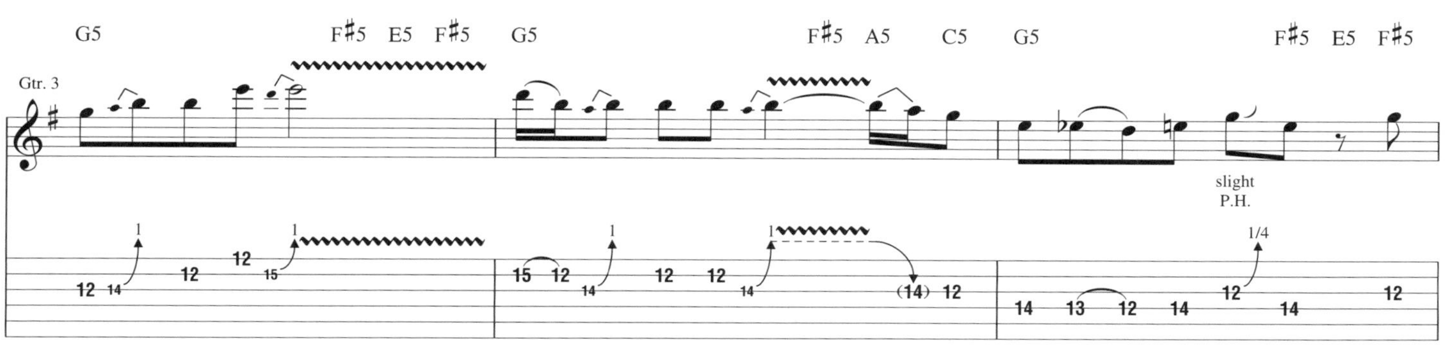
G5
F♯5 E5 F♯5
G5
F♯5 A5 C5
G5
F♯5 E5 F♯5
Gtr. 3
slight P.H.
1
1
1
1
1/4
12 14 12 12 15
15 12 14 12 12 14 (14) 12
14 13 12 14 12 14 12

G5
F♯5 A5 C5
E5
Gtr. 3 tacet
A load-ed gun, un - hap-py smile. He'll scope the free - way
slight P.H.
1/4
1
1/4
14 12 X 14 12 (12)
14 (14)

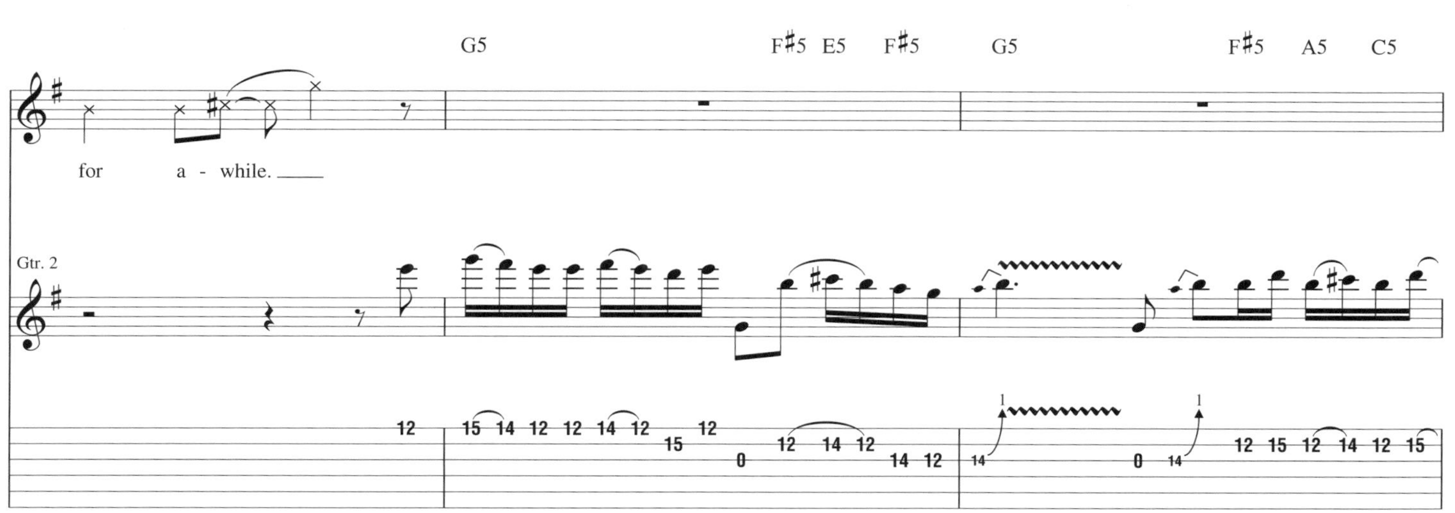
G5
F♯5 E5 F♯5
G5
F♯5 A5 C5
for a - while.
Gtr. 2
1
1
12
15 14 12 12 14 12 15 12 0 12 14 12 14 12
14 0 14 12 15 12 14 12 15

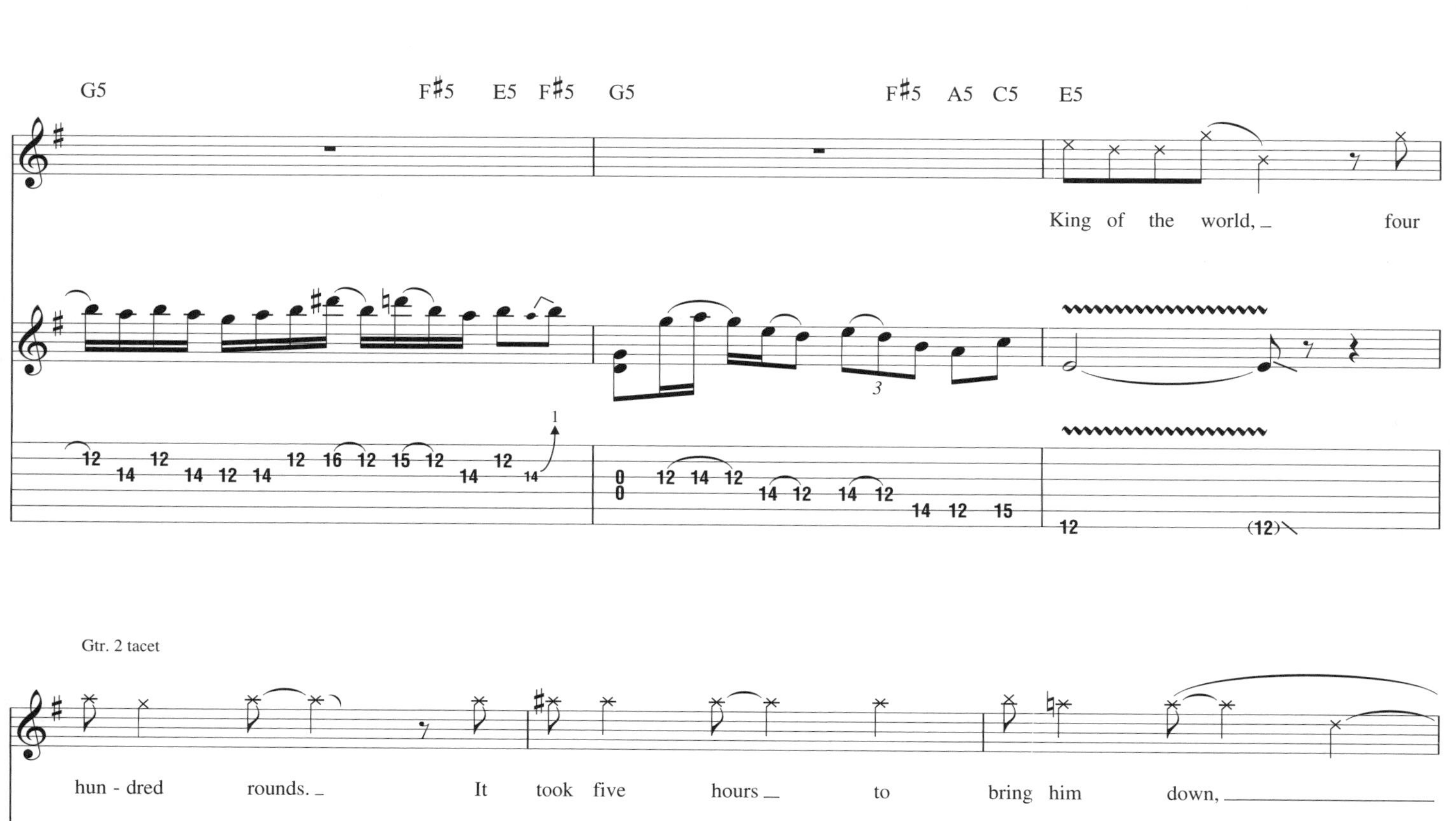

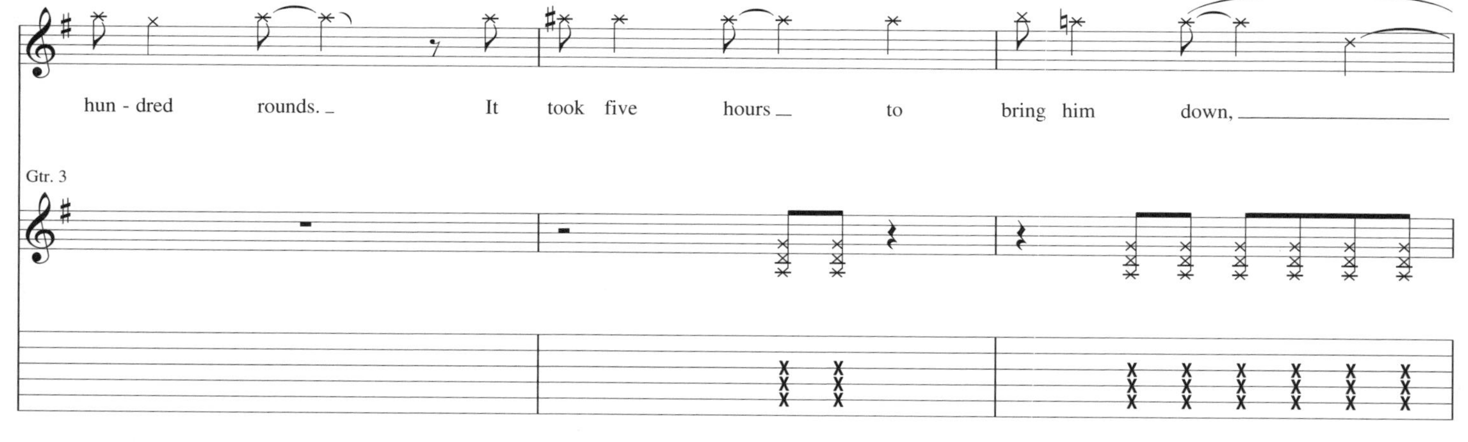

D.S. al Coda 2

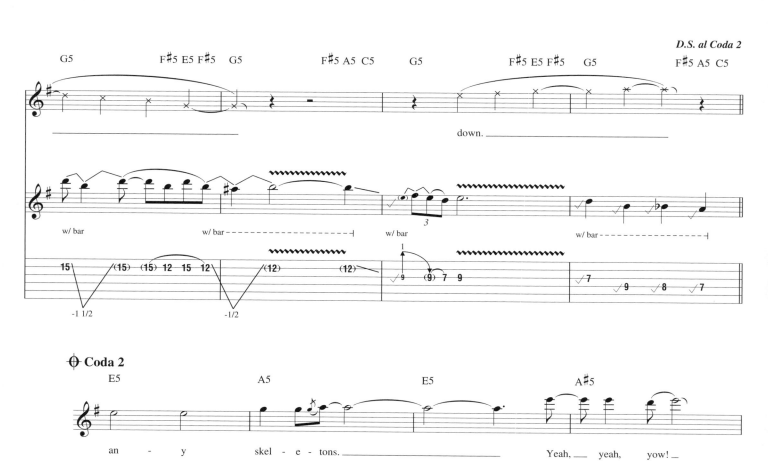

G5 F♯5 E5 F♯5 G5 F♯5 A5 C5 G5 F♯5 E5 F♯5 G5 F♯5 A5 C5

down.

w/ bar w/ bar w/ bar w/ bar

15 (15) (15) 12 15 12 (12) (12) 9 (9) 7 9 7 9 8 7

-1 1/2 -1/2

Coda 2

E5 A5 E5 A♯5

an - y skel - e - tons. Yeah, yeah, yow!

E5
A5
E5
A♯5
Look out!
Gtr. 2
8va
loco
1 hold bend
An - y skel - e - tons.
Yeah, yow!
Outro
Gtr. 1: w/ Rhy. Fig. 3
Gtr. 2 tacet
E5 F♯5 B5 A♯5
Ha, ha, ha, ha, ha.
Gtr. 1

from *We've Come for You All*

What Doesn't Die

Words and Music by Frank Bello, Charlie Benante, John Bush and Scott Rosenfeld

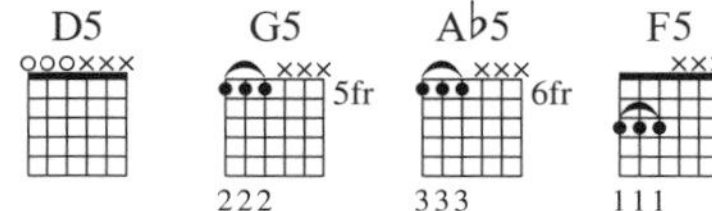

Drop D tuning, down 1/2 step:
(low to high) D♭-A♭-D♭-G♭-B♭-E♭

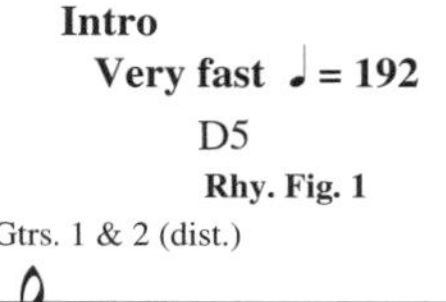

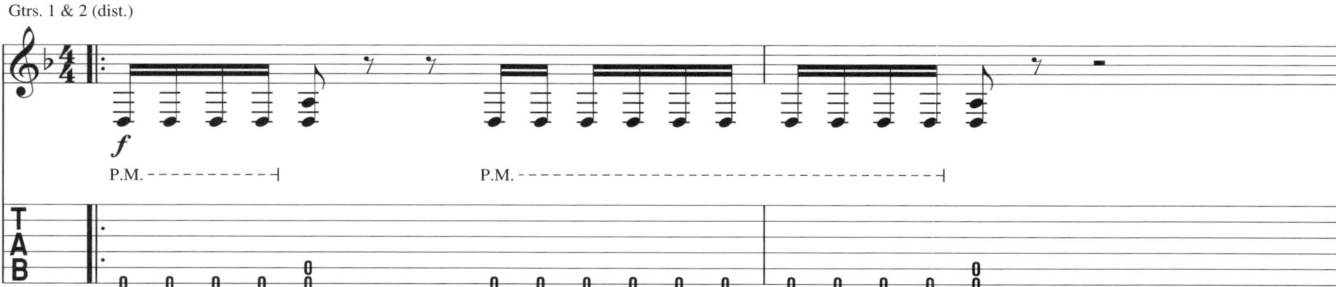

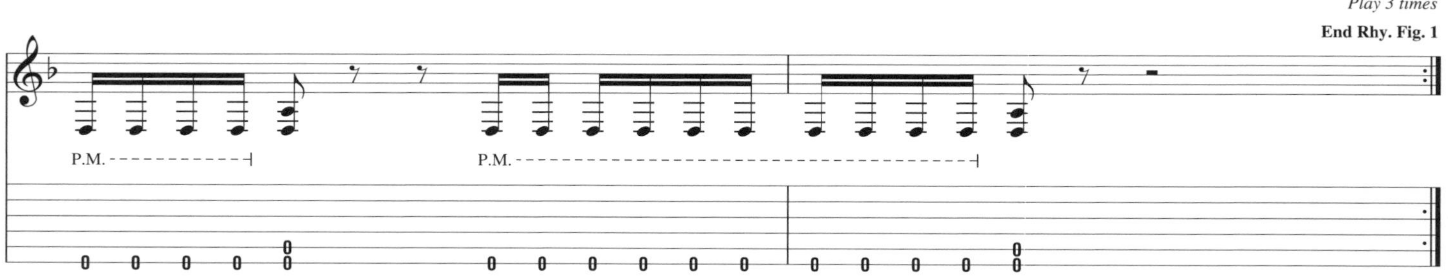

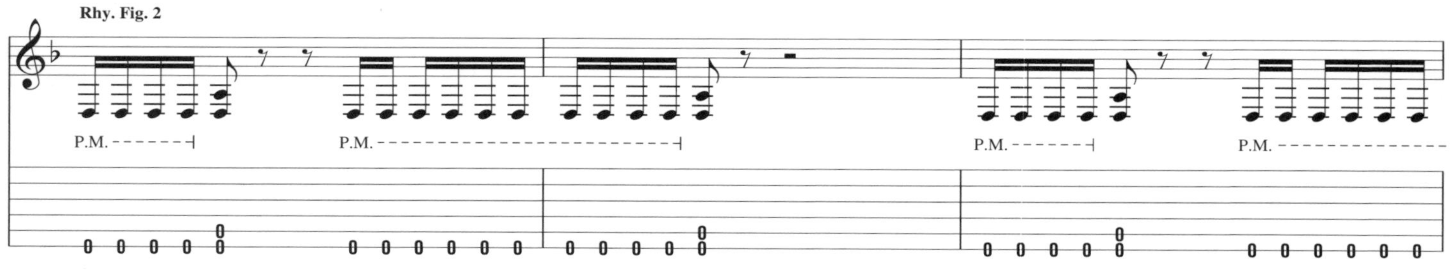

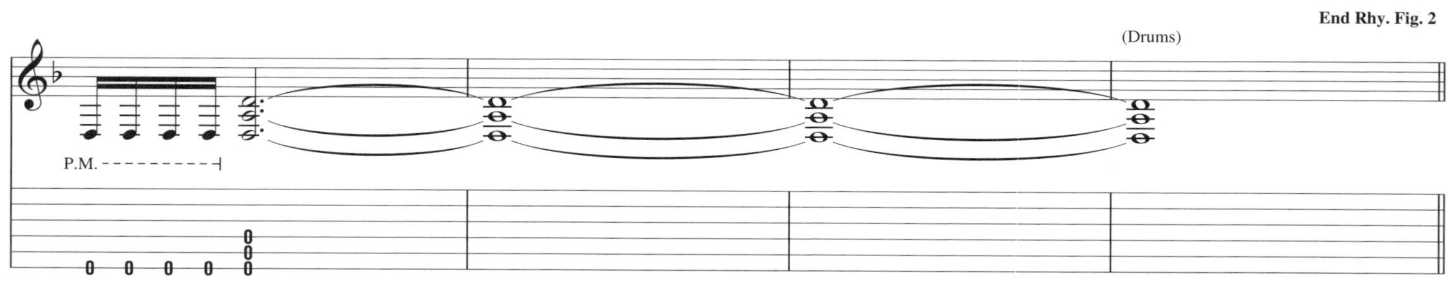

Verse
G5
Ab5
G5 F5
1. First in, last out, o - ver - thrown. It's been picked clean to the bone.
Rhy. Fig. 3
End Rhy. Fig. 3
P.M.
Gtrs. 1 & 2: w/ Rhy. Fig. 3 (3 times)
It's so hard to re-mem - ber things like when we used to kill our kings. Cru -
sad-ing for hy - poc - ri - sy. Un-der our nose the ho - ly bleed. Crum-bling un - der its
own weight, a - pol - o - gies if you re - late. 'Cause
8va
Gtr. 3 (dist.)
loco
fdbk.
*Vol. swell
Pitch: B
Chorus
Half-time feel
D5
Rhy. Fig. 4
Gtrs. 1 & 2
End Rhy. Fig. 4
you can - not kill what does-n't die.

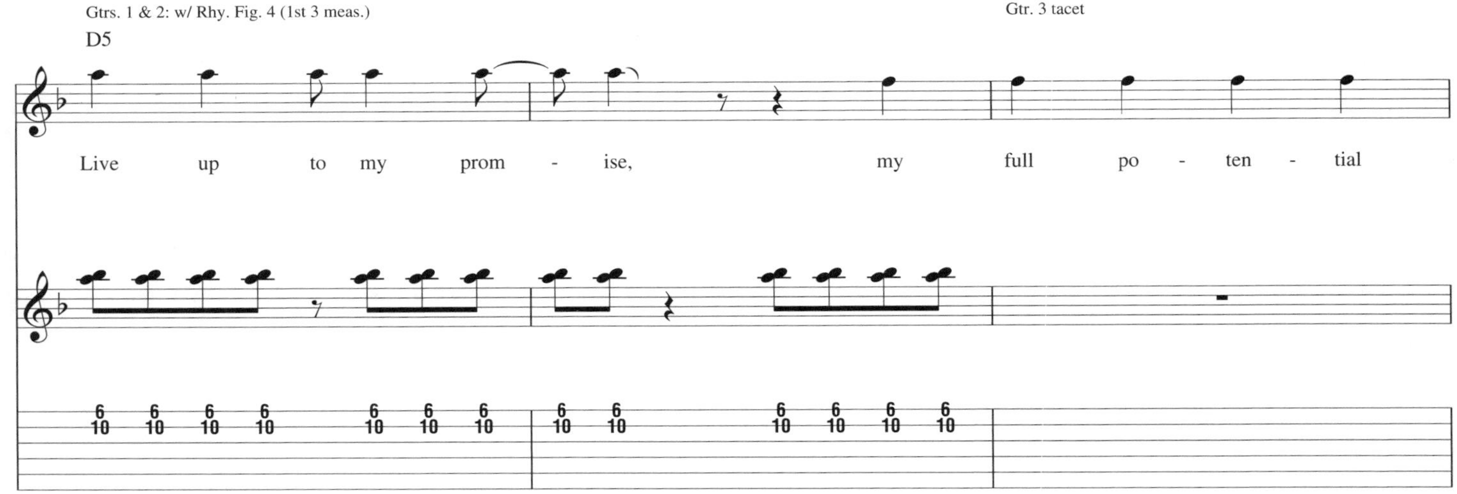
Gtrs. 1 & 2: w/ Rhy. Fig. 4 (1st 3 meas.)
Gtr. 3 tacet
D5
Live up to my prom - ise, my full po - ten - tial

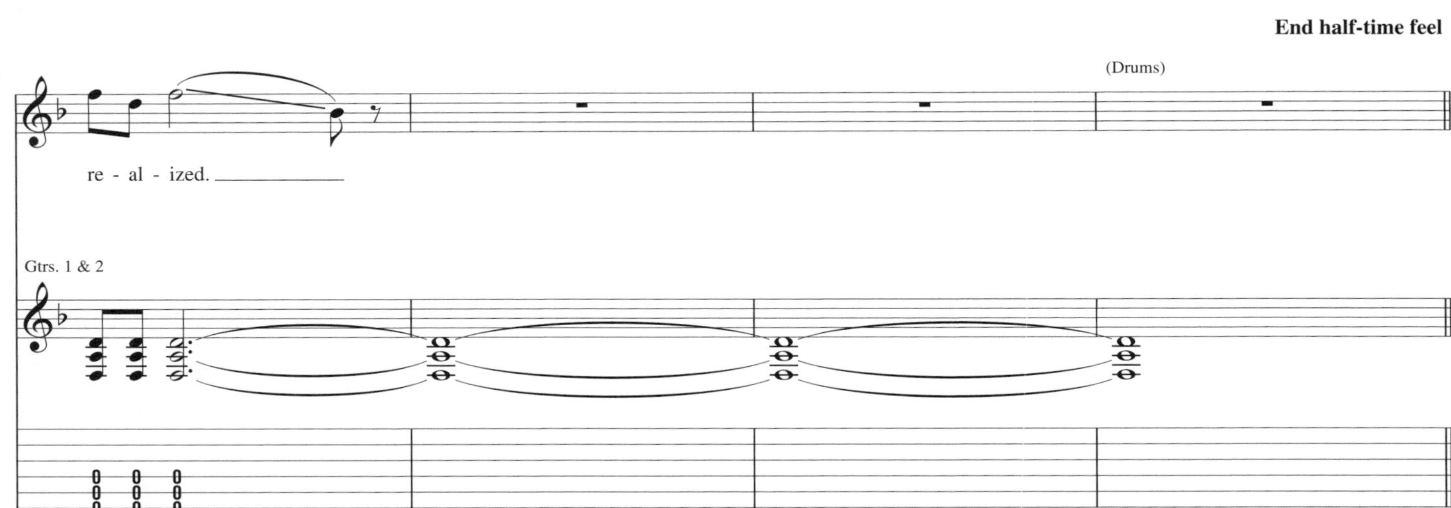
End half-time feel
(Drums)
re - al - ized.
Gtrs. 1 & 2

Verse

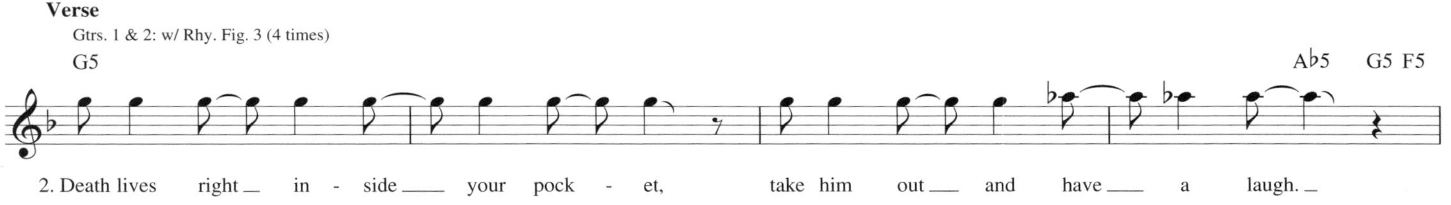
Gtrs. 1 & 2: w/ Rhy. Fig. 3 (4 times)
G5
A♭5 G5 F5
2. Death lives right in - side your pock - et, take him out and have a laugh.

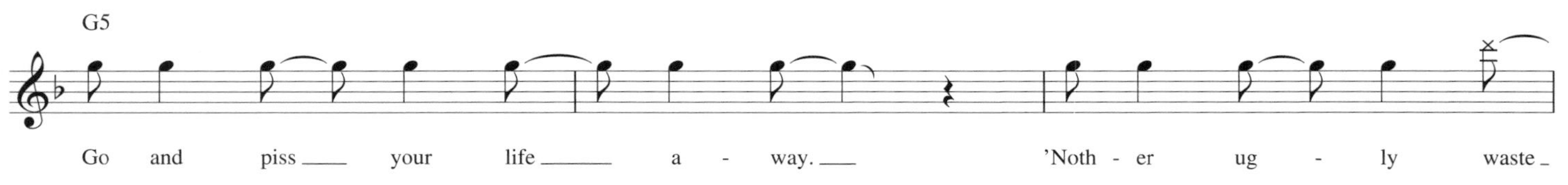
G5
Go and piss your life a - way. 'Noth - er ug - ly waste

A♭5 G5 F5 G5
of clay. And up a - bove there's no one home. Why don't you an - swer

Ab5 G5 F5 G5
Ab5 G5 F5
your phone? Re-mind-ing me to learn that poem. First in, last out, o-ver-thrown, be-cause
8va
Gtr. 3
fdbk.
mf
fdbk.
f
Pitch: C
*Vol. swell
Chorus
Half-time feel
Gtrs. 1 & 2: w/ Rhy. Fig. 4 (3 times)
D5 G5 Ab5 G5 F5
you can-not kill what does-n't die.
Riff A
loco
End Riff A
1st time, Gtr. 3: w/ Riff A
2nd time, Gtr. 3: w/ Riff A (2 times)
2nd time, End half-time feel
D5 G5 Ab5 G5 F5
Live up to my prom - ise, my full po - ten - tial re - al - ized.
To Coda
1st time, End half-time feel
D5 G5 Ab5 G5 F5
You can-not kill what does-n't die.
Gtr. 3

Free time

Gtrs. 1 & 2: w/ Rhy. Fig. 2

D5

Live up to my prom - ise, my full po - ten - tial re - al - ized.

8va

fdbk.

mf

Pitch: C♯

*Vol. swell

Interlude

Slower ♩ = 140

*Gtrs. 3 & 4: w/ random fdbk. & noise (next 16 meas.)

G5 A♭5 F5 G♭5 A♭5 F5 G5 A♭5 F5 G♭5 A♭5 F5

Rhy. Fig. 5

End Rhy. Fig. 5

Play 3 times

Gtrs. 1 & 2

*Gtr. 4 (dist.), played *f*.

Gtrs. 1 & 2: w/ Rhy. Fig. 5

G5 A♭5 F5 G♭5 A♭5 F5 G5 A♭5 F5 G♭5 A♭5 F5

Ah.

Bridge

D5

Stream of con - scious - ness flows in - to a riv - er of

Gtr. 1

Harm.

Pitch: D

*Harmonic located approximately three-tenths the distance between the 2nd & 3rd frets.

Gtr. 2

Harm.

Pitch: C D C

**Harmonic located approximately six-tenths the distance between the 2nd & 3rd frets.

***Harmonic located approximately three-tenths the distance between the 2nd & 3rd frets.

G5
A♭5
G5
F5
D5
blood.
Stem this tide of vi-
Gtr. 4
rake
1/2
Gtrs. 1 & 2
Gtr. 4 tacet
G5
A♭5
G5 F5
-o-lence
as it ris-es
like a flood.
Gtr. 4
1 1/2
Gtr. 5 (dist.)
w/ wah-wah
fdbk.
*Vol. swell
Gtr. 1
Harm.
Pitch: C D C
Gtr. 2
Harm.
Pitch: C A

Guitar Solo
Gtrs. 1 & 2: w/ Rhy. Fig. 5 (4 times)
G5
A♭5
F5
G♭5
Gtr. 5
hold bend
Harm.
Gtrs. 3 & 4: w/ random fdbk. & noise
8va

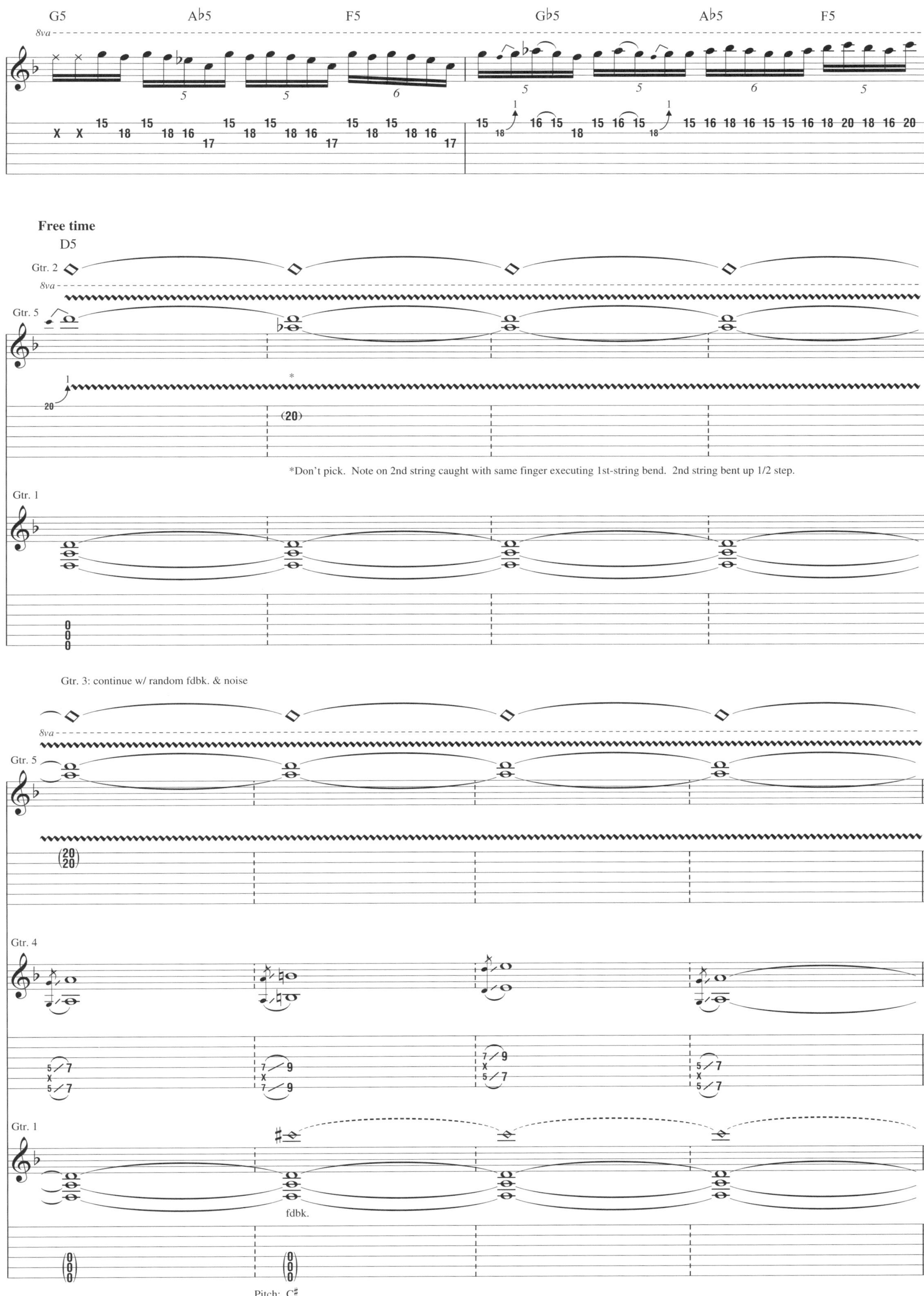
G5
A♭5
F5
G♭5
A♭5
F5
8va
Free time
D5
Gtr. 2
Gtr. 5
*Don't pick. Note on 2nd string caught with same finger executing 1st-string bend. 2nd string bent up 1/2 step.
Gtr. 1
Gtr. 3: continue w/ random fdbk. & noise
Gtr. 4
fdbk.
Pitch: C♯

Interlude
Tempo I

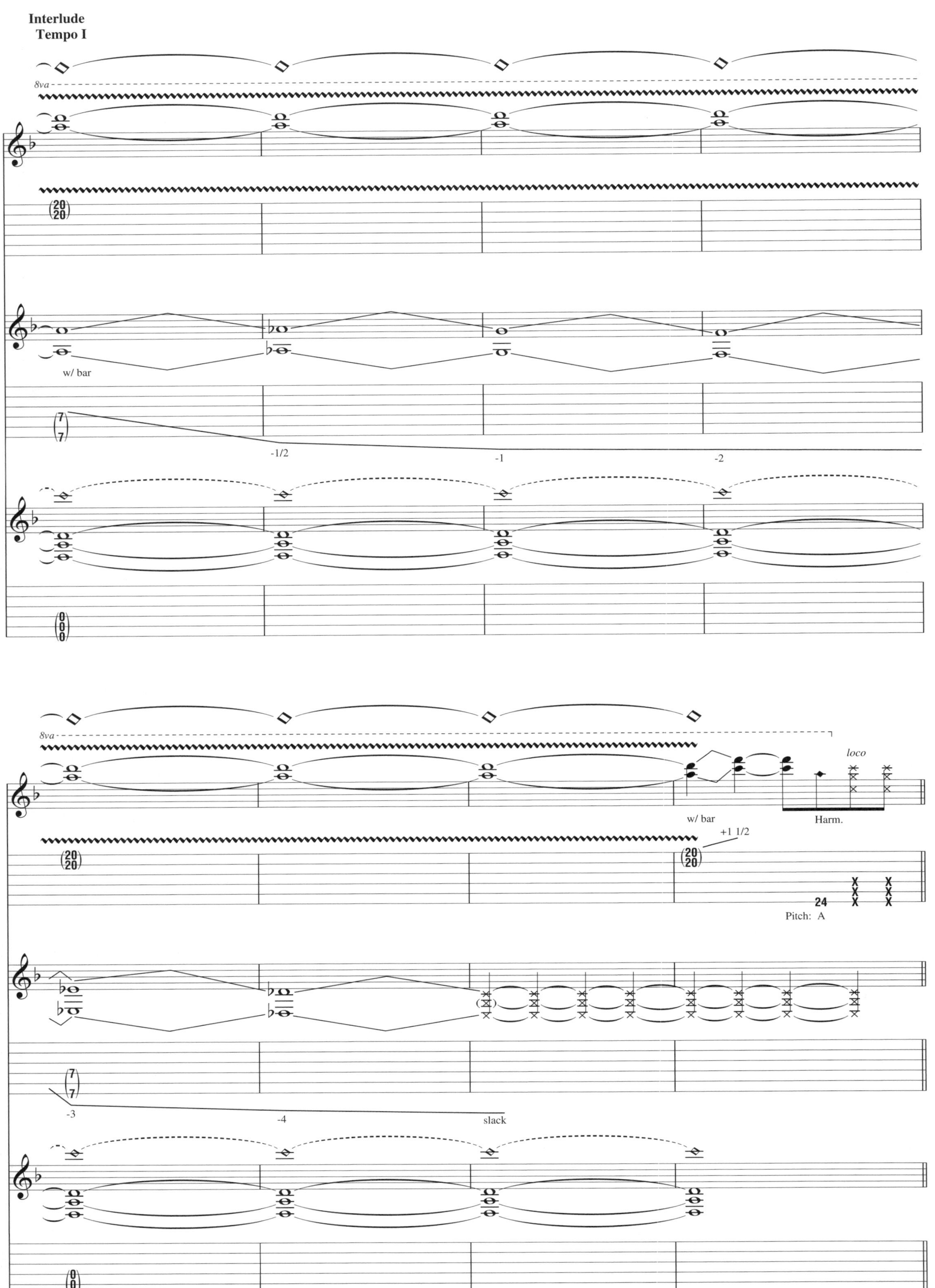

Bridge
Gtrs. 1 & 2: w/ Rhy. Fig. 1 (4 times)
Gtrs. 3, 4 & 5 tacet
D5
Stream of con - scious - ness flows in - to a riv - er of blood.
Stem this tide of vi - o - lence as it ris - es like a flood.
1.
2.
like a flood.
A stream of con - scious - ness flows in - to a riv - er of
Riff B
*Gtrs. 1 & 2
P.M.
*Composite arrangement
blood.
(What does - n't die.)
End Riff B
Gtrs. 1 & 2: w/ Riff B
Stem this tide of vi - o - lence as it ris - es like a flood.

A stream of con - scious - ness flows in - to a riv - er of
Gtrs. 1 & 2
P.M.
blood.
(What does - n't die.)
15ma
Gtr. 3
Harm.
2.3
Pitch: G
*Vol. swell
Gtrs. 1 & 2
P.M.
Stem this tide of vi - o - lence
15ma
mf
(2.3)
P.M.

D.S. al Coda
as it ris - es like a flood.
15ma
(2.3)
P.M.
Coda
D5
Live up to my prom - ise, my
Gtr. 3
Gtrs. 1 & 2
Gtr. 3 tacet
N.C.
full po - ten - tial re - al - ized.
Gtrs. 1 & 2
P.M.
P.M.

GUITAR NOTATION LEGEND

Guitar music can be notated three different ways: on a *musical staff*, in *tablature*, and in *rhythm slashes*.

RHYTHM SLASHES are written above the staff. Strum chords in the rhythm indicated. Use the chord diagrams found at the top of the first page of the transcription for the appropriate chord voicings. Round noteheads indicate single notes.

THE MUSICAL STAFF shows pitches and rhythms and is divided by bar lines into measures. Pitches are named after the first seven letters of the alphabet.

TABLATURE graphically represents the guitar fingerboard. Each horizontal line represents a string, and each number represents a fret.

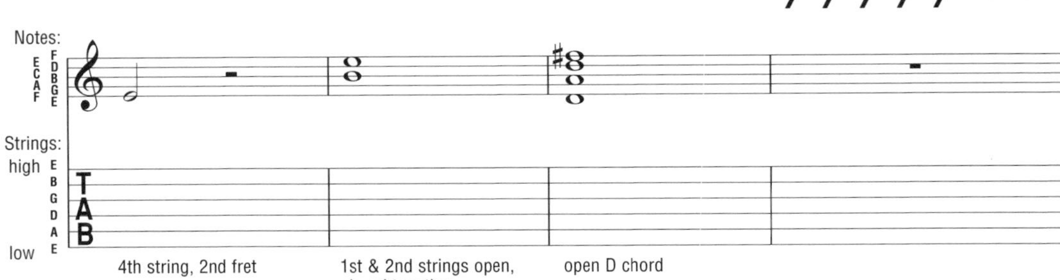

HALF-STEP BEND: Strike the note and bend up 1/2 step.

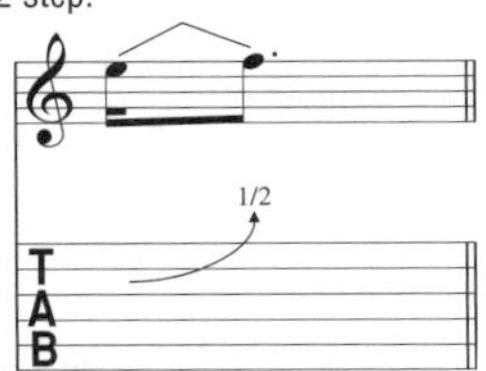

WHOLE-STEP BEND: Strike the note and bend up one step.

GRACE NOTE BEND: Strike the note and immediately bend up as indicated.

SLIGHT (MICROTONE) BEND: Strike the note and bend up 1/4 step.

BEND AND RELEASE: Strike the note and bend up as indicated, then release back to the original note. Only the first note is struck.

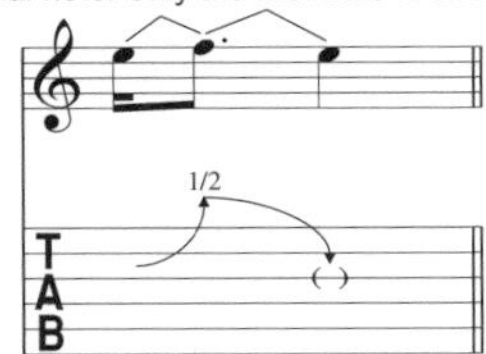

PRE-BEND: Bend the note as indicated, then strike it.

VIBRATO: The string is vibrated by rapidly bending and releasing the note with the fretting hand.

WIDE VIBRATO: The pitch is varied to a greater degree by vibrating with the fretting hand.

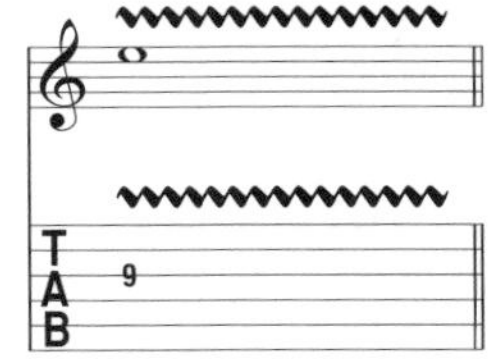

HAMMER-ON: Strike the first (lower) note with one finger, then sound the higher note (on the same string) with another finger by fretting it without picking.

PULL-OFF: Place both fingers on the notes to be sounded. Strike the first note and without picking, pull the finger off to sound the second (lower) note.

LEGATO SLIDE: Strike the first note and then slide the same fret-hand finger up or down to the second note. The second note is not struck.

SHIFT SLIDE: Same as legato slide, except the second note is struck.

TRILL: Very rapidly alternate between the notes indicated by continuously hammering on and pulling off.

TAPPING: Hammer ("tap") the fret indicated with the pick-hand index or middle finger and pull off to the note fretted by the fret hand.

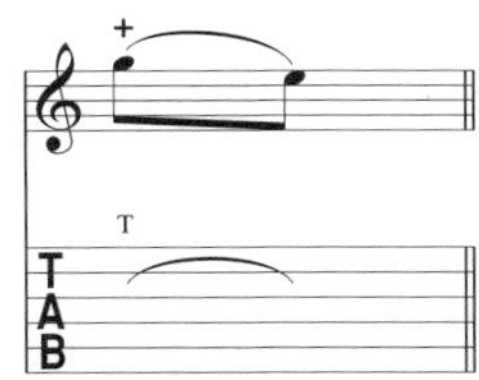

NATURAL HARMONIC: Strike the note while the fret-hand lightly touches the string directly over the fret indicated.

PINCH HARMONIC: The note is fretted normally and a harmonic is produced by adding the edge of the thumb or the tip of the index finger of the pick hand to the normal pick attack.

PICK SCRAPE: The edge of the pick is rubbed down (or up) the string, producing a scratchy sound.

MUFFLED STRINGS: A percussive sound is produced by laying the fret hand across the string(s) without depressing, and striking them with the pick hand.

PALM MUTING: The note is partially muted by the pick hand lightly touching the string(s) just before the bridge.

RAKE: Drag the pick across the strings indicated with a single motion.

TREMOLO PICKING: The note is picked as rapidly and continuously as possible.

VIBRATO BAR DIVE AND RETURN: The pitch of the note or chord is dropped a specified number of steps (in rhythm), then returned to the original pitch.

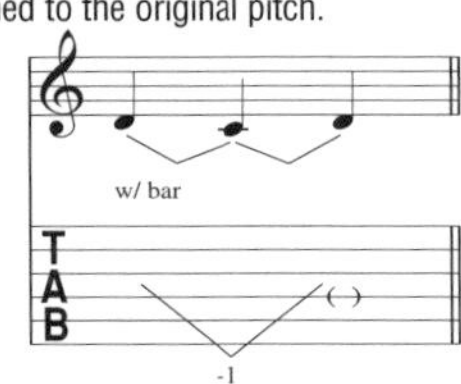

VIBRATO BAR SCOOP: Depress the bar just before striking the note, then quickly release the bar.

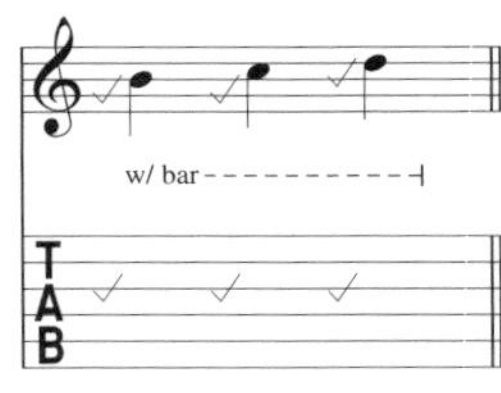

VIBRATO BAR DIP: Strike the note and then immediately drop a specified number of steps, then release back to the original pitch.

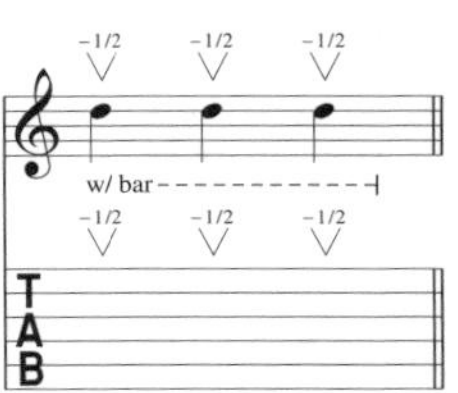

GUITAR RECORDED VERSIONS®

Guitar Recorded Versions® are note-for-note transcriptions of guitar music taken directly off recordings. This series, one of the most popular in print today, features some of the greatest guitar players and groups from blues and rock to country and jazz.

Guitar Recorded Versions are transcribed by the best transcribers in the business. Every book contains notes and tablature. Visit www.halleonard.com for our complete selection.

00690016 The Will Ackerman Collection $19.95
00690501 Bryan Adams – Greatest Hits $19.95
00690002 Aerosmith – Big Ones $24.95
00692015 Aerosmith – Greatest Hits $22.95
00690603 Aerosmith – O Yeah! (Ultimate Hits) $24.95
00690147 Aerosmith – Rocks $19.95
00690146 Aerosmith – Toys in the Attic $19.99
00690139 Alice in Chains $19.95
00690178 Alice in Chains – Acoustic $19.95
00694865 Alice in Chains – Dirt $19.95
00660225 Alice in Chains – Facelift $19.95
00694925 Alice in Chains – Jar of Flies/Sap $19.95
00690387 Alice in Chains – Nothing Safe: Best of the Box $19.95
00690899 All That Remains – The Fall of Ideals $19.95
00690812 All-American Rejects – Move Along $19.95
00690983 All-American Rejects – When the World Comes Down $22.99
00694932 Allman Brothers Band – Definitive Collection for Guitar Volume 1 $24.95
00694933 Allman Brothers Band – Definitive Collection for Guitar Volume 2 $24.95
00694934 Allman Brothers Band – Definitive Collection for Guitar Volume 3 $24.95
00690958 Duane Allman Guitar Anthology $24.99
00690945 Alter Bridge – Blackbird $22.99
00690755 Alter Bridge – One Day Remains $19.95
00690571 Trey Anastasio $19.95
00691013 The Answer – Everyday Demons $19.99
00690158 Chet Atkins – Almost Alone $19.95
00694876 Chet Atkins – Contemporary Styles $19.95
00694878 Chet Atkins – Vintage Fingerstyle $19.95
00690865 Atreyu – A Deathgrip on Yesterday $19.95
00690609 Audioslave $19.95
00690804 Audioslave – Out of Exile $19.95
00690884 Audioslave – Revelations $19.95
00690926 Avenged Sevenfold $22.95
00690820 Avenged Sevenfold – City of Evil $24.95
00694918 Randy Bachman Collection $22.95
00690366 Bad Company – Original Anthology – Book 1 $19.95
00690367 Bad Company – Original Anthology – Book 2 $19.95
00690503 Beach Boys – Very Best of $19.95
00694929 Beatles: 1962-1966 $24.95
00694930 Beatles: 1967-1970 $24.95
00690489 Beatles – 1 $24.99
00694880 Beatles – Abbey Road $19.95
00690110 Beatles – Book 1 (White Album) $19.95
00690111 Beatles – Book 2 (White Album) $19.95
00690902 The Beatles – The Capitol Albums, Volume 1 $24.99
00694832 Beatles – For Acoustic Guitar $22.99
00690137 Beatles – A Hard Day's Night $16.95
00690482 Beatles – Let It Be $17.95
00694891 Beatles – Revolver $19.95
00694914 Beatles – Rubber Soul $19.95
00694863 Beatles – Sgt. Pepper's Lonely Hearts Club Band $19.95
00690383 Beatles – Yellow Submarine $19.95
00690632 Beck – Sea Change $19.95
00694884 Best of George Benson $19.95
00692385 Chuck Berry $19.95
00690835 Billy Talent $19.95
00690879 Billy Talent II $19.95
00690149 Black Sabbath $14.95
00690901 Best of Black Sabbath $19.95
00690148 Black Sabbath – Master of Reality $14.95
00690142 Black Sabbath – Paranoid $14.95
00692200 Black Sabbath – We Sold Our Soul for Rock 'N' Roll $19.95
00690674 blink-182 $19.95
00690389 blink-182 – Enema of the State $19.95
00690831 blink-182 – Greatest Hits $19.95
00690523 blink-182 – Take Off Your Pants and Jacket $19.95
00690028 Blue Oyster Cult – Cult Classics $19.95
00690851 James Blunt – Back to Bedlam $22.95
00690008 Bon Jovi – Cross Road $19.95
00690827 Bon Jovi – Have a Nice Day $22.95
00690913 Boston $19.95
00690932 Boston – Don't Look Back $19.99
00690829 Boston Guitar Collection $19.99
00690491 Best of David Bowie $19.95
00690583 Box Car Racer $19.95
00690873 Breaking Benjamin – Phobia $19.95
00690764 Breaking Benjamin – We Are Not Alone $19.95
00690451 Jeff Buckley Collection $24.95
00690957 Bullet for My Valentine – Scream Aim Fire $19.95
00690678 Best of Kenny Burrell $19.95
00690564 The Calling – Camino Palmero $19.95
00690261 Carter Family Collection $19.95
00690043 Best of Cheap Trick $19.95
00690171 Chicago – The Definitive Guitar Collection $22.95
00691004 Chickenfoot $22.99
00691011 Chimaira Guitar Collection $24.99
00690567 Charlie Christian – The Definitive Collection $19.95
00690590 Eric Clapton – Anthology $29.95
00692391 Best of Eric Clapton – 2nd Edition $22.95
00690936 Eric Clapton – Complete Clapton $29.99
00690074 Eric Clapton – Cream of Clapton $24.95
00690247 Eric Clapton – 461 Ocean Boulevard $19.99
00690010 Eric Clapton – From the Cradle $19.95
00690716 Eric Clapton – Me and Mr. Johnson $19.95
00694873 Eric Clapton – Timepieces $19.95
00694869 Eric Clapton – Unplugged $22.95
00690415 Clapton Chronicles – Best of Eric Clapton $18.95
00694896 John Mayall/Eric Clapton – Bluesbreakers $19.95
00690162 Best of the Clash $19.95
00690828 Coheed & Cambria – Good Apollo I'm Burning Star, IV, Vol. 1: From Fear Through the Eyes of Madness $19.95
00690940 Coheed and Cambria – No World for Tomorrow $19.95
00690494 Coldplay – Parachutes $19.95
00690593 Coldplay – A Rush of Blood to the Head $19.95
00690906 Coldplay – The Singles & B-Sides $24.95
00690962 Coldplay – Viva La Vida $19.95
00690806 Coldplay – X & Y $19.95
00690855 Best of Collective Soul $19.95
00690928 Chris Cornell – Carry On $19.95
00694940 Counting Crows – August & Everything After $19.95
00690405 Counting Crows – This Desert Life $19.95
00694840 Cream – Disraeli Gears $19.95
00690285 Cream – Those Were the Days $17.95
00690352 Creed – My Own Prison $19.95
00690551 Creed – Weathered $19.95
00690819 Best of Creedence Clearwater Revival $22.95
00690648 The Very Best of Jim Croce $19.95
00690572 Steve Cropper – Soul Man $19.95
00690613 Best of Crosby, Stills & Nash $22.95
00690777 Crossfade $19.95
00699521 The Cure – Greatest Hits $24.95
00690637 Best of Dick Dale $19.95
00690941 Dashboard Confessional – The Shade of Poison Trees $19.95
00690892 Daughtry $19.95
00690822 Best of Alex De Grassi $19.95
00690967 Death Cab for Cutie – Narrow Stairs $22.99
00690289 Best of Deep Purple $17.95
00690288 Deep Purple – Machine Head $17.99
00690784 Best of Def Leppard $19.95
00694831 Derek and the Dominos – Layla & Other Assorted Love Songs $22.95
00692240 Bo Diddley – Guitar Solos by Fred Sokolow $19.99
00690384 Best of Ani DiFranco $19.95
00690322 Ani DiFranco – Little Plastic Castle $19.95
00690380 Ani DiFranco – Up Up Up Up Up Up $19.95
00690979 Best of Dinosaur Jr. $19.99
00690833 Private Investigations – Best of Dire Straits and Mark Knopfler $24.95
00695382 Very Best of Dire Straits – Sultans of Swing $19.95
00690347 The Doors – Anthology $22.95
00690348 The Doors – Essential Guitar Collection $16.95
00690915 Dragonforce – Inhuman Rampage $29.99
00690250 Best of Duane Eddy $16.95
00690533 Electric Light Orchestra Guitar Collection $19.95
00690909 Best of Tommy Emmanuel $19.95
00690555 Best of Melissa Etheridge $19.95
00690524 Melissa Etheridge – Skin $19.95
00690496 Best of Everclear $19.95
00690515 Extreme II – Pornograffitti $19.95
00690982 Fall Out Boy – Folie à Deux $22.99
00690810 Fall Out Boy – From Under the Cork Tree $19.95
00690897 Fall Out Boy – Infinity on High $22.95
00691009 Five Finger Death Punch $19.99
00690664 Best of Fleetwood Mac $19.95
00690870 Flyleaf $19.95
00690257 John Fogerty – Blue Moon Swamp $19.95
00690931 Foo Fighters – Echoes, Silence, Patience & Grace $19.95
00690235 Foo Fighters – The Colour and the Shape $19.95
00690808 Foo Fighters – In Your Honor $19.95
00690595 Foo Fighters – One by One $19.95
00690394 Foo Fighters – There Is Nothing Left to Lose $19.95
00690805 Best of Robben Ford $19.95
00690842 Best of Peter Frampton $19.95
00690734 Franz Ferdinand $19.95
00694920 Best of Free $19.95
00690222 G3 Live – Joe Satriani, Steve Vai, and Eric Johnson $22.95
00694807 Danny Gatton – 88 Elmira St $19.95
00690438 Genesis Guitar Anthology $19.95
00690858 David Gilmour – On an Island $24.95
00690753 Best of Godsmack $19.95
00120167 Godsmack $19.95
00690848 Godsmack – IV $19.95
00690338 Goo Goo Dolls – Dizzy Up the Girl $19.95
00690576 Goo Goo Dolls – Gutterflower $19.95
00690773 Good Charlotte – Chronicles of Life and Death $19.95
00690601 Good Charlotte – The Young and the Hopeless $19.95
00690927 Patty Griffin – Children Running Through $19.95
00690591 Patty Griffin – Guitar Collection $19.95
00690978 Guns N' Roses – Chinese Democracy $24.99
00694854 Buddy Guy – Damn Right, I've Got the Blues $19.95
00690697 Best of Jim Hall $19.95
00690840 Ben Harper – Both Sides of the Gun $19.95
00690987 Ben Harper and Relentless7 – White Lies for Dark Times $22.99
00694798 George Harrison Anthology $19.95
00690778 Hawk Nelson – Letters to the President $19.95
00690841 Scott Henderson – Blues Guitar Collection $19.95
00692930 Jimi Hendrix – Are You Experienced? $24.95
00692931 Jimi Hendrix – Axis: Bold As Love $22.95
00690304 Jimi Hendrix – Band of Gypsys $24.99
00690321 Jimi Hendrix – BBC Sessions $22.95
00690608 Jimi Hendrix – Blue Wild Angel $24.95
00694944 Jimi Hendrix – Blues $24.95
00692932 Jimi Hendrix – Electric Ladyland $24.95
00690602 Jimi Hendrix – Smash Hits $24.99
00690017 Jimi Hendrix – Woodstock $24.95
00690843 H.I.M. – Dark Light $19.95
00690869 Hinder – Extreme Behavior $19.95
00660029 Buddy Holly $19.95
00690793 John Lee Hooker Anthology $24.99
00660169 John Lee Hooker – A Blues Legend $19.95
00694905 Howlin' Wolf $19.95
00690692 Very Best of Billy Idol $19.95
00690688 Incubus – A Crow Left of the Murder $19.95
00690457 Incubus – Make Yourself $19.95
00690544 Incubus – Morningview $19.95
00690136 Indigo Girls – 1200 Curfews $22.95
00690790 Iron Maiden Anthology $24.99
00690887 Iron Maiden – A Matter of Life and Death $24.95
00690730 Alan Jackson – Guitar Collection $19.95
00694938 Elmore James – Master Electric Slide Guitar $19.95
00690652 Best of Jane's Addiction $19.95
00690721 Jet – Get Born $19.95
00690684 Jethro Tull – Aqualung $19.95
00690693 Jethro Tull Guitar Anthology $19.95
00690647 Best of Jewel $19.95
00690898 John 5 – The Devil Knows My Name $22.95
00690959 John 5 – Requiem $22.95
00690814 John 5 – Songs for Sanity $19.95
00690751 John 5 – Vertigo $19.95

00694912 Eric Johnson – Ah Via Musicom $19.95
00690660 Best of Eric Johnson $19.95
00690845 Eric Johnson – Bloom $19.95
00690169 Eric Johnson – Venus Isle $22.95
00690846 Jack Johnson and Friends – Sing-A-Longs and Lullabies for the Film Curious George $19.95
00690271 Robert Johnson – The New Transcriptions $24.95
00699131 Best of Janis Joplin $19.95
00690427 Best of Judas Priest $22.99
00690651 Juanes – Exitos de Juanes $19.95
00690277 Best of Kansas $19.95
00690911 Best of Phil Keaggy $24.99
00690727 Toby Keith Guitar Collection $19.99
00690742 The Killers – Hot Fuss $19.95
00690888 The Killers – Sam's Town $19.95
00690504 Very Best of Albert King $19.95
00690444 B.B. King & Eric Clapton – Riding with the King $19.95
00690134 Freddie King Collection $19.95
00690975 Kings of Leon – Only by the Night $22.99
00690339 Best of the Kinks $19.95
00690157 Kiss – Alive! $19.95
00694903 Best of Kiss for Guitar $24.95
00690355 Kiss – Destroyer $16.95
14026320 Mark Knopfler – Get Lucky $22.99
00690164 Mark Knopfler Guitar – Vol. 1 ....$19.95
00690163 Mark Knopfler/Chet Atkins – Neck and Neck $19.95
00690930 Korn $19.95
00690780 Korn – Greatest Hits, Volume 1 ....$22.95
00690836 Korn – See You on the Other Side $19.95
00690377 Kris Kristofferson Collection $19.95
00690861 Kutless – Hearts of the Innocent $19.95
00690834 Lamb of God – Ashes of the Wake $19.95
00690875 Lamb of God – Sacrament $19.95
00690977 Ray LaMontagne – Gossip in the Grain $19.99
00690890 Ray LaMontagne – Till the Sun Turns Black $19.95
00690823 Ray LaMontagne – Trouble $19.95
00690658 Johnny Lang – Long Time Coming $19.95
00690726 Avril Lavigne – Under My Skin $19.95
00690679 John Lennon – Guitar Collection $19.95
00690781 Linkin Park – Hybrid Theory $22.95
00690782 Linkin Park – Meteora $22.95
00690922 Linkin Park – Minutes to Midnight $19.95
00690783 Best of Live $19.95
00699623 The Best of Chuck Loeb $19.95
00690743 Los Lonely Boys $19.95
00690720 Lostprophets – Start Something $19.95
00690525 Best of George Lynch $24.99
00690955 Lynyrd Skynyrd – All-Time Greatest Hits $19.99
00694954 New Best of Lynyrd Skynyrd $19.95
00690577 Yngwie Malmsteen – Anthology $24.95
00694845 Yngwie Malmsteen – Fire and Ice $19.95
00694755 Yngwie Malmsteen's Rising Force $19.95
00694757 Yngwie Malmsteen – Trilogy $19.95
00690754 Marilyn Manson – Lest We Forget $19.95
00694956 Bob Marley – Legend $19.95
00690548 Very Best of Bob Marley & The Wailers – One Love $22.99
00694945 Bob Marley – Songs of Freedom $24.95
00690914 Maroon 5 – It Won't Be Soon Before Long $19.95
00690657 Maroon 5 – Songs About Jane $19.95
00690748 Maroon 5 – 1.22.03 Acoustic $19.95
00690989 Mastodon – Crack the Skye $22.99
00690442 Matchbox 20 – Mad Season $19.95
00690616 Matchbox Twenty – More Than You Think You Are $19.95
00690239 Matchbox 20 – Yourself or Someone like You $19.95
00690382 Sarah McLachlan – Mirrorball $19.95
00120080 The Don McLean Songbook $19.95
00694952 Megadeth – Countdown to Extinction $22.95
00690244 Megadeth – Cryptic Writings $19.95
00694951 Megadeth – Rust in Peace $22.95
00690011 Megadeth – Youthanasia $19.95
00690505 John Mellencamp Guitar Collection $19.95
00690562 Pat Metheny – Bright Size Life $19.95
00690646 Pat Metheny – One Quiet Night $19.95
00690559 Pat Metheny – Question & Answer $19.95
00690040 Steve Miller Band Greatest Hits $19.95
00690769 Modest Mouse – Good News for People Who Love Bad News $19.95
00694802 Gary Moore – Still Got the Blues $22.99
00691005 Best of Motion City Soundtrack $19.99
00690787 Mudvayne – L.D. 50 ....$22.95
00690996 My Morning Jacket Collection $19.99
00690984 Matt Nathanson – Some Mad Hope $22.99
00690500 Ricky Nelson Guitar Collection $17.95
00690722 New Found Glory – Catalyst $19.95
00690880 New Found Glory – Coming Home $19.95
00690611 Nirvana $22.95
00694895 Nirvana – Bleach $19.95
00690189 Nirvana – From the Muddy Banks of the Wishkah $19.95
00694913 Nirvana – In Utero $19.95
00694901 Nirvana – Incesticide $19.95
00694883 Nirvana – Nevermind $19.95
00690026 Nirvana – Unplugged in New York $19.95
00120112 No Doubt – Tragic Kingdom $22.95
00690121 Oasis – (What's the Story) Morning Glory $19.95
00690226 Oasis – The Other Side of Oasis $19.95
00690358 The Offspring – Americana $19.95
00690485 The Offspring – Conspiracy of One $19.95
00690203 The Offspring – Smash $18.95
00690818 The Best of Opeth $22.95
00694847 Best of Ozzy Osbourne $22.95
00690921 Ozzy Osbourne – Black Rain $19.95
00694830 Ozzy Osbourne – No More Tears $19.95
00690399 Ozzy Osbourne – The Ozzman Cometh $19.95
00690129 Ozzy Osbourne – Ozzmosis $22.95
00690933 Best of Brad Paisley $22.95
00690995 Brad Paisley – Play: The Guitar Album $24.99
00690866 Panic! At the Disco – A Fever You Can't Sweat Out $19.95
00690885 Papa Roach – The Paramour Sessions $19.95
00690939 Christopher Parkening – Solo Pieces $19.99
00690594 Best of Les Paul $19.95
00694855 Pearl Jam – Ten $19.95
00690439 A Perfect Circle – Mer De Noms $19.95
00690661 A Perfect Circle – Thirteenth Step $19.95
00690725 Best of Carl Perkins $19.99
00690499 Tom Petty – Definitive Guitar Collection $19.95
00690868 Tom Petty – Highway Companion $19.95
00690176 Phish – Billy Breathes $22.95
00690331 Phish – Story of the Ghost $19.95
00690428 Pink Floyd – Dark Side of the Moon $19.95
00690789 Best of Poison $19.95
00693864 Best of The Police $19.95
00690299 Best of Elvis: The King of Rock 'n' Roll $19.95
00692535 Elvis Presley $19.95
00690003 Classic Queen $24.95
00694975 Queen – Greatest Hits $24.95
00690670 Very Best of Queensryche $19.95
00690878 The Raconteurs – Broken Boy Soldiers $19.95
00694910 Rage Against the Machine $19.95
00690179 Rancid – And Out Come the Wolves $22.95
00690426 Best of Ratt $19.95
00690055 Red Hot Chili Peppers – Blood Sugar Sex Magik $19.95
00690584 Red Hot Chili Peppers – By the Way $19.95
00690379 Red Hot Chili Peppers – Californication $19.95
00690673 Red Hot Chili Peppers – Greatest Hits $19.95
00690090 Red Hot Chili Peppers – One Hot Minute $22.95
00690852 Red Hot Chili Peppers – Stadium Arcadium $24.95
00690893 The Red Jumpsuit Apparatus – Don't You Fake It $19.95
00690511 Django Reinhardt – The Definitive Collection $19.95
00690779 Relient K – MMHMM $19.95
00690643 Relient K – Two Lefts Don't Make a Right ... But Three Do $19.95
00694899 R.E.M. – Automatic for the People $19.95
00690260 Jimmie Rodgers Guitar Collection $19.95
00690014 Rolling Stones – Exile on Main Street $24.95
00690631 Rolling Stones – Guitar Anthology $27.95
00690685 David Lee Roth – Eat 'Em and Smile $19.95
00690031 Santana's Greatest Hits $19.95
00690796 Very Best of Michael Schenker $19.95
00690566 Best of Scorpions $19.95
00690604 Bob Seger – Guitar Anthology $19.95
00690659 Bob Seger and the Silver Bullet Band – Greatest Hits, Volume 2 ....$17.95
00690896 Shadows Fall – Threads of Life $19.95
00690803 Best of Kenny Wayne Shepherd Band $19.95
00690750 Kenny Wayne Shepherd – The Place You're In $19.95
00690857 Shinedown – Us and Them $19.95
00690196 Silverchair – Freak Show $19.95
00690130 Silverchair – Frogstomp $19.95
00690872 Slayer – Christ Illusion $19.95
00690813 Slayer – Guitar Collection $19.95
00690419 Slipknot $19.95
00690973 Slipknot – All Hope Is Gone $22.99
00690530 Slipknot – Iowa $19.95
00690733 Slipknot – Volume 3 (The Subliminal Verses) $22.99
00690330 Social Distortion – Live at the Roxy $19.95
00120004 Best of Steely Dan $24.95
00694921 Best of Steppenwolf $22.95
00690655 Best of Mike Stern $19.95
00690021 Sting – Fields of Gold $19.95
00690597 Stone Sour $19.95
00690689 Story of the Year – Page Avenue $19.95
00690520 Styx Guitar Collection $19.95

AUTHENTIC TRANSCRIPTIONS WITH NOTES AND TABLATURE

00120081 Sublime $19.95
00690519 SUM 41 – All Killer No Filler $19.95
00690994 Taylor Swift $22.99
00690993 Taylor Swift – Fearless $22.99
00690767 Switchfoot – The Beautiful Letdown $19.95
00690425 System of a Down $19.95
00690830 System of a Down – Hypnotize $19.95
00690799 System of a Down – Mezmerize $19.95
00690531 System of a Down – Toxicity $19.95
00694824 Best of James Taylor $16.95
00694887 Best of Thin Lizzy $19.95
00690671 Three Days Grace $19.95
00690871 Three Days Grace – One-X $19.95
00690737 3 Doors Down – The Better Life $22.95
00690891 30 Seconds to Mars – A Beautiful Lie $19.95
00690665 Thursday – War All the Time $19.95
00690030 Toad the Wet Sprocket $19.95
00690654 Best of Train $19.95
00690233 The Merle Travis Collection $19.99
00690683 Robin Trower – Bridge of Sighs $19.95
00699191 U2 – Best of: 1980-1990 ....$19.95
00690732 U2 – Best of: 1990-2000 ....$19.95
00690894 U2 – 18 Singles $19.95
00690775 U2 – How to Dismantle an Atomic Bomb $22.95
00690997 U2 – No Line on the Horizon $19.99
00690039 Steve Vai – Alien Love Secrets $24.95
00690172 Steve Vai – Fire Garden $24.95
00660137 Steve Vai – Passion & Warfare $24.95
00690881 Steve Vai – Real Illusions: Reflections $24.95
00694904 Steve Vai – Sex and Religion $24.95
00690392 Steve Vai – The Ultra Zone $19.95
00690024 Stevie Ray Vaughan – Couldn't Stand the Weather $19.95
00690370 Stevie Ray Vaughan and Double Trouble – The Real Deal: Greatest Hits Volume 2 ....$22.95
00690116 Stevie Ray Vaughan – Guitar Collection $24.95
00660136 Stevie Ray Vaughan – In Step $19.95
00694879 Stevie Ray Vaughan – In the Beginning $19.95
00660058 Stevie Ray Vaughan – Lightnin' Blues '83-'87 ....$24.95
00690036 Stevie Ray Vaughan – Live Alive $24.95
00694835 Stevie Ray Vaughan – The Sky Is Crying $22.95
00690025 Stevie Ray Vaughan – Soul to Soul $19.95
00690015 Stevie Ray Vaughan – Texas Flood $19.95
00690772 Velvet Revolver – Contraband $22.95
00690920 Velvet Revolver – Libertad $19.95
00690132 The T-Bone Walker Collection $19.95
00694789 Muddy Waters – Deep Blues $24.95
00690071 Weezer (The Blue Album) $19.95
00690516 Weezer (The Green Album) $19.95
00690286 Weezer – Pinkerton $19.95
00690447 Best of the Who $24.95
00694970 The Who – Definitive Guitar Collection: A-E $24.95
00694971 The Who – Definitive Guitar Collection F-Li $24.95
00694972 The Who – Definitive Guitar Collection: Lo-R $24.95
00694973 The Who – Definitive Guitar Collection: S-Y $24.95
00690672 Best of Dar Williams $19.95
00690319 Stevie Wonder – Some of the Best $17.95
00690596 Best of the Yardbirds $19.95
00690696 Yeah Yeah Yeahs – Fever to Tell $19.95
00690844 Yellowcard – Lights and Sounds $19.95
00690916 The Best of Dwight Yoakam $19.95
00690904 Neil Young – Harvest $19.95
00690443 Frank Zappa – Hot Rats $19.95
00690623 Frank Zappa – Over-Nite Sensation $19.95
00690589 ZZ Top – Guitar Anthology $24.95
00690960 ZZ Top Guitar Classics $19.99

For More Information, See Your Local Music Dealer, Or Write To:

7777 W. Bluemound Rd. P.O. Box 13819 Milwaukee, WI 53213

Complete songlists and more at **www.halleonard.com**
Prices, contents, and availability subject to change without notice.

0110